D0676787

TOO MUCH COLLEGE

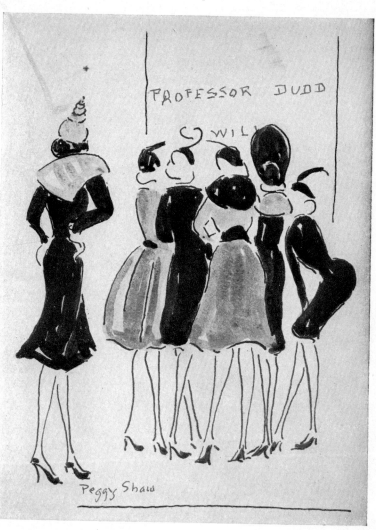

COLLEGE CALLING

Stephen Leacock

Too Much College

OR

Education Eating Up Life

*With Kindred Essays in
Education and Humour*

785

Dodd, Mead & Company
New York   1942

CONTENTS

CONTENTS

EPILOGUE

PREFACE

THIS book is based on an experience of nearly twenty years of school and college training, ten years of school-teaching, thirty-six years of college lecturing, and three years of retirement, to think it over. The opinion that I have reached is that education, in the narrow sense of school and college attendance, is taking too heavy a toll of the years of life and that the curriculum should be shortened. But, in the wider sense, what I want to advocate is not to make education shorter, but to make it much longer—indeed to make it last as long as life itself.

What I find wrong is the stark division now existing between the years of formal education and entry into the work of life. Education has become to a great extent a mere acquirement of a legal qualification to enter a closed profession, in place of being a process undertaken for its own sake. All that is best in education can only be acquired by spontaneous interest; thus gained it lasts and goes on. Education merely imposed as a compulsory prerequisite to something else finishes and withers when its task is done. Real education should mean a wonderful beginning, a marvellous initiation, a thorough "smattering," and life will carry it on.

A part of the present difficulty is that our school and college curriculum in its one thousand years of development from the church schools of the Middle Ages has taken on a mass of subject matter beyond the range of any one mind. We have not yet learned to condense to useful essentials the things beyond study in detail. The best part of any subject is the general view, the thorough smattering just mentioned, that carries to the individual the results for which others have given the work of their lives. The outline of the world's history can occupy half an hour, or half a session, or half a century.

We have further encumbered the curriculum with the attempt to teach things that cannot be imparted by classroom work—too practical for anything but actual practice, or too vague and general for anything but general reflection.

Nor is it only the subject matter of the curriculum that needs reduction. A saving of time perhaps equally important can be effected by altering the form and method of its progress. To a very great extent all our school children and students in America and in England move along in a system of one-year promotions, all advancing together—or staying back to join the next consignment.

Thus, by the time the student has reached middle high school on his way to college, he has already joined a sort of "convoy" that moves slowly down the widening stream of education, always at the pace of the slowest. It sweeps along majestically, working puzzles, muttering declensions, answering quizzes and translating *"parlez-vous."*

Any ordinary bright boy could strike out from the convoy, like a sloop from a fleet, like a fast motor boat from among freighters, and distance it by two years.

By the time the heavy convoy reached its goal, he would have been there already for years, married, with one and a half children, an established position, whiskers, debts, life. He would watch the convoy discharging its spectacled neophytes, thirty years old, timid in the daylight, shuddering at life, having lived for thirty years on other people's money. That's a little exaggerated, but it's good enough.

The practical person asks how we are supposed to bring about this vastly altered program. To abolish overnight our whole system of examinations, promotions and graded classes moving all together would leave our education a hopeless mess. And to this the only answer is that there is nothing that we can do about it, nothing particular and all of a minute.

It is our current fault always to think in terms of deliberate regulation and ordinance. We seek to accomplish friendship with a league, Mother's Day with a statute, welcome with a by-law and sobriety with a code. Without the spirit, all falls in a littered heap. If education is to change, there must first come the consciousness of the need of change.

STEPHEN LEACOCK

Professor Emeritus McGill University, B.A. (Toronto), Ph.D. (Chicago), Litt.D. (Brown, Dartmouth and Toronto), LL.D. (Queen's and McGill), D.C.L. (Bishop's).

McGill University
October 1, 1939

TOO MUCH COLLEGE

I

Education Eating Up Life

CHAPTER I

EDUCATION EATING UP LIFE

Education longer and longer — Life ten years too late, and Death on time — Where we got our Curriculum — Mediaeval Schools with Modern Extension — A Scholar and a Gentleman, plus a Scientist and a Business Man — The Straws on the Camel's Back

In this discussion of education, I am addressing myself to plain people. By this I mean people who shudder at mathematics, go no further in Latin than *E Pluribus Unum* and take electricity as they find it. As opposed to these are the academic class who live in colleges, or in the shadow of them, and claim education as their province. But the plain people are of necessity interested in education because their sons and daughters go to college, or, more important, can't go to college.

Now the plain people have noticed that education is getting longer and longer. Fifty years ago people learned to read out of a spelling-book at six years old, went to high school at twelve, and taught school (for money) on a third-class certificate at sixteen. After that, two years in a saw-mill and two at a medical school made them doctors, or one year in a saw-mill and one in divinity fitted them for the church. For law they needed no college at all, just three summers on a farm and three winters in an office.

All our great men in North America got this education. Pragmatically, it worked. They began their real life still young. With the money they didn't spend they bought a wife. By the age of thirty they had got somewhere, or nowhere. It is true that for five years of married life, they carried, instead of a higher degree, bills for groceries, coal, doctors and babies' medicine. Then they broke out of the woods, into the sunlight, established men—at an age when their successors are still demonstrating, interning, or writing an advanced thesis on social impetus.

Now it is all changed. Children in school at six years old cut up paper dolls and make patterns. They are still in high school till eighteen, learning civics and social statistics—studies for old men. They enter college at about nineteen or twenty, take prerequisites and post-requisites in various faculties for nearly ten years, then become demonstrators, invigilators, researchers, or cling to a graduate scholarship like a man on a raft.

At thirty they are just beginning, ten years too late. They can't marry till it's ten years too late; they have children ten years too late, and die ten years too early. They know nothing of the early life of the man who worked in saw-mills, practiced medicine at twenty and married six months later, with no other property than a stethoscope and a horse and buggy; or of the young lawyer who married in debt, and lived happy in it ever after.

"Safety first" has put its stamp on life. Population

begins to die at the top. And, all the time, education grows longer and longer. This does not deny that the average human life is now longer. It means that paternity is shorter. People do not see enough of their grandchildren—the sweetest prospect in the world. Life has all too little evening. It has all run in arrears and never catches up.

All this, you will say, is exaggerated, is overcolored, is not truth. Very likely. But a half truth in argument, like a half brick, carries better. High colors show up where neutral tints blend to nothing. Yet the main truth gets over. Education is eating up life.

In the above paragraphs I have formulated the plain man's accusations against the continued lengthening of education; or, rather, I must not say his accusation. The poor fellow hasn't the spirit to accuse. It is not an accusation that he formulates or a grievance that he voices. It is just a burden that he carries.

He carries it because of the prestige of education. Round the idea of education, as effort and opportunity, there have clustered centuries of tradition and association. These are stamped in such words and phrases as "the little red schoolhouse," "the midnight oil," "the eager student," "the kindly dominie," "the absent-minded professor." With this has grown up the notion —no doubt partly true—that the harder the path of learning the higher the achievement. "There is no royal road to learning" still cheers those who are unaware that the public road itself has become overgrown with a jungle of underbrush.

In other words, people don't complain. On the contrary, they are often proud of the burden that they carry. Parents have no regrets for the fifteen years of sacrifice that they made to give their children the education they should have had in half the time.

It is a tradition with us that education opens opportunity. To send a boy to college is an ambition that wakes to life beside a cradle. "How is your son doing at school, Mr. McGregor?" I once asked of a Scotsman of the traditional type. "Fine!" he answered. "If he keeps on as he is, we'll have to put the college to him."

Even in the clutter and failure of youth's career among the blocked avenues of our misfit world the college comes into its own as a sort of refuge. "My son," said another parent, "doesn't seem to have any particular ability, so we think we'll have to send him to college. He seems no good for anything else." The one anxiety of such parents is, "Can he get in?" Beyond that no need to look. It's like being dipped in the Jordan.

But even if the plain man were to raise his complaint against the lengthening road and the increasing burden, he would be laughed out of court by the academic class. He would be told that our education is all too short. The teachers in the high schools would say that the children come to them hopelessly unprepared and ought to stay a year longer in public school.

Every professor will tell them that the first-year students at college are simply hopeless and ought to have stayed at least a year, or call it two, at high school. The students in the second year ought never to have left the first; the third-year men haven't the proper grounding for their work; and the fourth-year are so rotten that they have to be given degrees to get rid of them. As for the graduate school, the students in it should never have been admitted; they are not yet fit for advanced work. Their minds are immature. And even when they do get out of the graduate school, by sheer lapse of time, it seems ridiculous to think of them as fit to teach, or do anything. Oh, no; they have to go to Germany for a year—anyway, to somewhere for a year—and come back with whiskers and look like something.

I once put the question of shortening the college curriculum to my old friend Dean Elderberry Foible, dean of the Faculty of Arts. You didn't know him, but there was a dean at your college just like him. "Preposterous," he said, "preposterous!" And that settled it.

If we turn from the general view to the particular subjects, the case against any attempt to shorten the curriculum becomes simply overwhelming—so much so that we are crushed and humbled in presenting it. Imagine trying to leave out mathematics—the queen of sciences; or history—the very basis for understanding our modern life; or English literature—our legacy common to England and America, dear as the very hearthstones of our homes—who dares touch that?

Or who will dare disturb Latin, the bedrock of our culture; or foreign languages, the amenity of polite life; or geology, deep as the caverns of thought; biology, life's interpretation; or the social sciences, the key to the padlock of happiness still closed. Help! Nothing but pretentious ignorance could suggest leaving out anything. As to any shortening, ask again my friend Dean Elderberry Foible and he will tell you that you can't. "My dear sir, you may wish to, but you simply can't"—with that academic finality with which professors dismiss the ideas of students.

So it appears even to ourselves on a first survey. Take mathematics. How can you shorten the subject? That stern struggle with the multiplication table, for many people not yet ended in victory, how can you make it less? Square root, as obdurate as a hardwood stump in a pasture—nothing but years of effort can extract it. You can't hurry the process.

Or pass from arithmetic to algebra: you can't shoulder your way past quadratic equations or ripple through the binomial theorem. Indeed, the other way; your feet are impeded in the tangled growth, your pace slackens, you sink and fall somewhere near the binomial theorem with the calculus in sight on the horizon. So died, for each of us, still bravely fighting, our mathematical training; except only for a set of people called "mathematicians"—born so, like crooks. Yet would we leave mathematics out? No, we hold our cross.

Latin too: do you want your son to grow up not knowing what a *sine qua non* is, and who wrote Virgil's *Aeneid?* Then he not only needs the whole present curriculum but more! At present the student learns just enough Latin not to be able to read it; he stops short of the saturation point—just gets wet with it and no more.

But why recite the entire list? The same truth holds, for the academic profession, of every one of the subjects of the school and college course. The student is not saturated, when he ought really to be soaked.

A parallel resistance blocks the pathway leading to the professions. The idea of any immediate entry into them, for a young man just out of college is ridiculous. A hundred years ago a man just out of college looked as good as a coin fresh from the mint, a sickle from the whetstone. At twenty-seven he was a Member of Congress, had four or five children, owned three or four thousand dollars' worth of property in his own right—and owed five thousand dollars. But nowadays! Imagine trusting a serious case of illness to a young fellow of twenty-seven barely out of college, and till yesterday an interne in a hospital. Out of the question!

And, later, when at last his turn comes, it is but a brief acme of success, and then, all of a sudden, it seems people are saying, "He's too old for the job, losing his grip—in fact, he's nearly fifty." He's an "old doctor"—once a term of esteem and confidence but now equivalent to an "old horse."

Thus in our ill-fit world youth and age jostle and hurry one another together—too young and then too old. Those who follow gardening know that green peas are first too young to pick and then, overnight as it seems, too old to eat. So with our educated people. Homer long ago said, "As is the race of leaves, so is the race of men." Make it college graduates and garden peas and it still holds good.

How did all this come about? Our system of education arose out of the mediaeval Latin schools of the church. It still carries, like a fossil snake in a stone, the mark of its original structure. Not that this was the earliest kind of education. But the others were different. Greek education included music and dancing and what we call the arts. It was supposed to fit people to live. Mediaeval education was supposed to fit people to die. Any school-boy of today can still feel the effect of it.

Greek education was free from the problems that have beset our own. It didn't include the teaching of languages, the Greeks despising all foreigners as barbarians. It avoided everything "practical" like the plague, and would have regarded a professor of Engineering as a child of the devil, misusing truth. Mathematics, crippled by the want of symbols, became a sort of dream—intense, difficult and proudly without purpose. Greek education carried with it no "exams" and "tests" for entry to the professions. A Greek dentist didn't have to pass in Latin. He used a hammer.

Thus philosophy, "the love of knowledge," came into its own, in talk as endless as on the porch of a Kentucky country store.

"Scholars" would deny the truth of this summary and talk of Archimedes, the world's first engineer, and Hippocrates, its earliest physician. But the proof of what I say is that Archimedes found no followers and Hippocrates waited five hundred years for Galen. Scholars always see exceptions where a plain man sees an even surface. But even a billiard ball, if you look close enough, is all covered with bumps.

Our education, then, comes down to us from the schools of the Middle Ages. These were organized by the church and the first aim was piety, not competence; the goal was the reading of the Scriptures and by that the salvation of the soul. On this basis, Alfred the Great planned schools for Saxon England. So, too, in France did Charlemagne, who couldn't read or write and felt a religious admiration for those who could—the same as an oil magnate of today feels toward a university.

So presently the monastic schools arose, and from their oriel windows came forth among the elm trees the sound of Latin chants intoned by choristers; and in the silent scriptorium the light from a stained window fell on the quiet "copyist" rewriting, letter by letter, in pigment upon parchment, "In the beginning was the Word." Thus passed monastic life in its quiet transition to Eternity.

These were the earliest schools—secluded, scholarly —born ancient like the "old-fashioned" children of aging parents. For the date, place them anywhere in the four hundred years from Alfred and Charlemagne to the days of Oxford and Paris.

These later schools—Oxford, Paris, and such— came when study no longer taught people how to die and keep out of hell, but how to live, as lawyers— two ambitions with an obvious relationship. Law hatched out under the wings of the church, as a duck hatches under a hen, later to horrify its parent.

Here again the vertebrate structure is still seen in the rock. Lincoln's Inn and Grey's Inn were originally, in a sense, works of God, the defunct Doctors Commons till its end a spirituality. Law, in England at least, struggled long before it shook off the hand of ghostly guidance. Even now the connection between law and religion remains in the quantity of oaths by which the business of the law secures its righteousness.

So there came, then, such schools as Oxford and Paris, which seem to have been at first huge random gatherings of students—mediaeval exaggeration puts 30,000 at Oxford in pre-record days. They had, before printing, hardly any books, and no examinations. The curriculum ran to endless discussion—more Kentucky. These "disputations" begot "tests" and awards (degrees) and brought into the world that child of sin, the written examination. A few odd people like Roger Bacon began digging into black knowledge about gunpowder, and so forth, and got put into jail for it. The lamp of learning still fell only on the Kingdom of Light, with lawyers dancing in the shadow.

The curriculum of these schools, the bedrock on which ours still rest, was the famous trinity of study, the Trivium, which meant grammar, rhetoric and logic; to this was supplemented the four further studies called the Quadrivium—music, arithmetic, geometry and astronomy. All were based on the use of Latin; they comprehended the whole circuit of human knowledge, and the supreme purpose of it all was salvation. The monk Alcuin, who was Charlemagne's "specialist" in education, has described for us how he taught his students:

> *To some I administer the honey of the sacred writings; others I try to inebriate with the wine of the ancient classics. I begin the nourishment of some with the apples of grammatical subtlety. I strive to illuminate many by the arrangement of the stars, as from the painted roof of a lofty palace.*

The whole extent of human knowledge was still within human comprehension. In our own day we meet men who think they "know it all." In the Middle Ages there were men who were sure they did. Of course, where knowledge ended superstition began, and that was infinite.

It was this curriculum which in the course of centuries has been expanded beyond recognition like the toad in Aesop that would be an ox. And still it has not burst. It drags along its huge amorphous outline, flabby as a dinosaur, over fifteen years of life.

Here is what happened to expand it. The revival of learning resuscitated Greek, a study forgotten by all but the Arabs. The rising kingdoms that replaced feudalism brought national States and set people to learning one another's languages. The English, having forgotten French, had to learn it again. Italian became "polite." Milton suggested that one ought to learn it, "in an odd hour." Modern languages were still not a part of education, but a sort of annex; so they remained till yesterday in England where all Englishmen

were supposed to "know French" from a governess
and a copy of Ollendorff's *Grammar* and a trip to
Boulogne. But, till yesterday, Eton, Rugby and Oxford never heard of it.

Printing, once in real use, expanded both opportunity and obligation. Students henceforth had books.
Contacts with the Arabs revealed a system of decimal
notation that made arithmetic a reality and algebra a
power. Mathematics in the time of the Stuarts, with
logarithms and the calculus, ceased to be a dream.
Physics converted Alcuin's wonder of the sky into class-
room formulae.

But even though mathematics in the sixteen hun-
dreds, in the days of Newton and Descartes, had become a real and intensive study—far transcending in
reach and in difficulty anything within the range of the
ordinary college man of today—it was still regarded
rather as an annex to learning than as learning itself.
The place of priority still lay with classical study, with
the literature of Greece and Rome. In this America
was a faithful child of England. Our earliest college
education was stamped with Roman letters, and its
passion for the Bible in the wilderness made it even
revert somewhat to the mediaeval type. The rules that
were promulgated in 1642 for admission to Harvard
College lay down the qualification thus:—

*When any scholar is able to understand Tully or
such like classical Latin author* extempore, *and to make
and speak true Latin in verse and prose,* suo ut aiunt
Marte: *and to decline perfectly the paradigms of nouns*

and verbs in the Greek tongue: let him then and not
before be capable of admission into the college.

For readers whose Latinity has slipped away from
them, let it be explained that Tully is not Irish, but
means Cicero. Earlier generations properly called Romans by their names, and not, as we have come to
do, with many of them, by their nicknames. Tully was
called "Cicero" (or bean-head) as one of us might be
called "Shorty." Harvard Latin in 1642 was still un-
defiled.

On the terms indicated few of us now would get
into Harvard. Fewer still would get out, since, for
that, every scholar had to be

"found able to read the originals of the Old and New
Testaments into the Latin tongue and to resolve them
logically: withal being of godly life and conversation."

On the outside edge or fringe of the classical studies,
of which mathematics and logic formed an adjunct,
were such things as natural philosophy, destined to vast
and rapid expansion, but of which the classical doctors
of divinity remained ignorant.

By the time of Queen Anne, some scholars already
admitted that they didn't know everything—not many,
though, or at least they qualified it by saying that what
they didn't know wasn't worth knowing.

What they referred to by this last phrase was this
natural philosophy, the new range of knowledge that
the eighteenth century was gathering, item by item,
fact by fact. These grew into the sciences of life—

botany and zoology, later to get their true name of
biology. Reverend classical scholars, full to the throat
with declensions, set them aside as a disturbance of
the Book of Genesis. But they wouldn't down.

Beside them grew, equally despised by the classicists,
the electric science drawn by Franklin from the clouds,
the oxygen distilled by Priestley from water, the geology of Lyell, dug up from what was once called Hades.
All the world knows the story. Within another hundred years a vast series of studies known as the natural sciences—at first opposed, derided and left to
mechanics and steam-engine drivers—broke at last the
barriers of the schools and flooded wide over the curriculum.

But the barriers, in England at least, did not break
until the waters had risen high and the pressure had
become overwhelming. In the middle nineteenth century, as Professor Huxley complained, the so-called
public schools had still a curriculum of the Middle
Ages.

*Until a few years back [he wrote in 1893], a boy
might have passed through any one of the great public schools with the greatest distinction and credit and
might never so much as heard of modern geography,
modern history and modern literature, of the English
language as a language, or of the whole circle of the
sciences, physical, moral and social; might never have
heard that the earth goes round the sun; that England
underwent a great revolution in 1688 and France another in 1789; that there once lived certain notable*

men called Chaucer, Shakespeare, Milton, Voltaire, Goethe, Schiller.

With this protest of common sense went a certain protest of spite—as against aristocratic culture by those unable to share it. Witness Herbert Spencer's diatribe against "The Education of a Gentleman."

Men dress their children's minds as they do their bodies in the prevailing fashion. As the Orinoco Indian puts on his paint before he leaves his hut . . . so a boy's drilling in Latin and Greek is insisted on, not because of their intrinsic value, but that he may not be disgraced by being found ignorant of them—that he may have the education of a gentleman.

But when at last the barriers broke, the new science came in a flood, till every high school student, in America more even than in England, turned alchemist, and every class-room sputtered with electricity. And with this, in the colleges first and spreading downwards to the schools, came a still newer set of studies—the social studies, economics and politics, the mingled brood of happiness and despair, of progress and poverty that Mill and Spencer and such people let loose upon the world. So deeply have they spread that little children learn "civics" first and find out what it means after; and so widely that the Japanese have studied it from Europe and teach it to the Chinese.

And as if civics and social welfare were not enough for the already overburdened curriculum, a chariot creaking up the rough slope of Parnassus, "Business,"

in the form of schools of commerce, must needs leap
on top of the load. It handed so heavy a tip to the
driver that it could not be put off, and more than that
it began to demand that the oldest and most respectable of the passengers be thrown out to make room for
it.

.   .   .   .

So there we stand, or rather move slowly onward,
the ascent of Parnassus turned into a ten years' journey during which the passengers must amuse themselves as best they may with the cards and dice of
college activities.

.   .   .   .   .   .

Meantime it is only to be expected that the conditions of the journey react upon the minds of the passengers. In other words it is only natural that this vast
burden of an increasing curriculum sets up a reaction
in the minds of the pupil and the student. From their
earliest years they become accustomed to reckon up
the things that they have done and finished with.
"We've finished Scripture," says a little girl in a child's
school; "we had it last year." For her the mould of
religious thought is all set. Don't ask her the names of
the twelve Apostles. She's had them—last year. She
is not responsible for the Apostles any more. So does
the high school student count up his years still needed
for matriculation as eagerly as a mariner measures his
distance to the shore. The college student opens his
career by classing himself not according to the year
in which he enters but according to the year in which
he hopes to get out. The class matriculating in 1940

call out in their infant breath, "Rah! Rah! Forty-four."

How strange it is, our little procession of life! The child says, "When I am a big boy." But what is that? The big boy says, "When I grow up." And then, grown up, he says, "When I get married." But to be married, what is that after all? The thought changes to "When I'm able to retire." And then, when retirement comes, he looks back over the landscape traversed; a cold wind seems to sweep over it; somehow he has missed it all, and it is gone. Life, we learn too late, is in the living, in the tissue of every day and hour. So it should be with education.

But so it is not; a false view discolours it all. For the vastly great part of it the student's one aim is to get done with it. There comes a glad time in his life when he has "finished" mathematics, a happy day when he has done philosophy, an exhilarating hour when he realizes that he is finished with "compulsory English." Then at last his four years are out, his sentence expired, and he steps out of college a free man, without a stain on his character—and not much on his mind. . . . Later on, he looks back wistfully and realizes how different it might have been.

.   .   .   .

It is the purpose of this book in the chapters that follow to discuss this discrepancy between education and life. The field of education here discussed is that of "general education" and the liberal arts which occupy about twenty years of the life of the great majority of college students. The work of technical and

professional schools—engineering, medicine and law—
lies apart. Here the adaptation of the means to the
end is sufficiently direct to lessen the danger of wandering into the wilderness as liberal arts has done.

This wandering into the wilderness has made the
journey of education too long, too cumbersome and
too expensive. Worse still, at the end of its wandering it comes to a full stop. The road comes to an end
just when it ought to be getting somewhere. The passengers alight, shaken and weary, to begin, all over
again, something else.

II

The Machine At Work

CHAPTER II

THE MACHINE AT WORK

*Strategic progress: no advance without security —
Spelling costs two years — Classes and credits; the
moving convoy — The end of the pavement, of examinations — History finds a magic mirror — Need
of a thorough smattering of science — And of a snug
corner of ignorance*

I AM a familiar guest in a household where there is a
little girl, now rapidly lengthening into a big girl, who
is attending what is called a ladies' school. In return
for help with Latin sentences and such things, I get
much casual information about what educationalists
call class method. I said to this young scholar the
other day, "I thought, June, you were in the fifth
declension?"

"We were before Xmas," June answered, "but *she's*
gone back to the second. We're reviewing."

She is, of course, the teacher, and where she leads,
June and her associates follow. I gather that their
education in Latin takes the form of a series of forward rushes, from which they fall back and entrench
themselves again on safe ground. A year ago at Easter
they reached the passive voice, only to be beaten clear
back out of it again. They are now reconsidering *amo*
and closing up the ranks for a new attack. But as the

23

term ends there will be a regular *review* in which they will fall steadily back toward the beginning of the book. Last year she gave them some prepositions, but there has since been a retreat that has entrenched them behind the safe lines of *bonus.*

The same method, I gather from June, is pursued in algebra. Last year they got as far as equations, but the ground proved shaky under their feet and *he* (mathematics is masculine) took them back for a review of factors and division. They needed, he said, more drill. They are drilling now and getting ready for the big algebraical mid-term review that will shove them clear backward out of the book—to re-form in the shelter of arithmetic.

At the beginning of each new term, of course, there is full review of last year's work—at the very time, perhaps, when the class below are in a bold forward skirmish into next year's work. Thus do June and her companions drift back and forward, like a star cluster moving among the constellations. In the course of time they will fortuitously drift out of the ladies' school into college—a sudden effort and over the top. Meantime they seem to move around in a circle, like fish in a trap, among quadratic equations and moods and tenses, going past the same opening of salvation again and again and not seeing it.

It is their expectation that, when they get into the enchanted waters called college, they will swim right on. But not so. Ask any first-year student in Arts in the month of October what he is doing, and he will say that they are not doing anything much yet. The professor is "revising." After Xmas he will be "reviewing" and by April they will pretty well be back to matriculation. There will be no advance without security. The second year will then review the work of the first, and so on. In a graduate school the students revise their undergraduate work, and admission to a Ph.D. degree, as I recall it, involves a general review of everything since the cradle.

.   .   .   .

Here then is the educational machine at work, grinding its way up the long slope of Parnassus, from its first loading up its freight of little children, all fluttering with kindergarten ribbons, till it finally stops among the debris and slag piles marked END OF TRACK, where it lets out its sad-eyed Ph.D.'s, looking for a job, five years too late, and engaged to be married five years later.

.   .   .   .

The first jolt in this upward ascent is when the children start to learn to spell and strike our crazy alphabet. Look what happens.

The eager child begins "N—O, no." "S—O, so." "All right so far," thinks the child—like the man who fell out of the high window. Indeed, it's more than all right. The thing is a pleasure. "N—O, no." "S—O, so," with a good hiss on the letter S. "It's a delight," says the child. "Show me more of it." In fact the logic of it has all the appeal that goes with what is called "the inevitable" in art.

Then something happens. "D—O, do," says the teacher, and a lifetime of trouble begins. Forty years later, the child, grown up but still unable to spell, will be calling to his wife from his writing-desk: "Mary, how do you spell 'dough'? I mean what you make bread with."

But there, I refuse to discuss phonetic spelling. It's too wearisome. People get tired at the mention of it. They themselves have learned to spell, or pretty nearly, and look on spelling as part of the troubles of childhood, like measles and Sunday school and having to obey father. They don't suspect that there is coiled up in it the loss of perhaps two years of human life.

If spelling were rational, universal and authoritative, an intelligent child would, in a month, be able to read any word that it could say. After that it would spell by reading. Best of all, it would enter at once into the magic garden that reading opens up. When one realizes the endless hours, the tears, the bad marks, the soiled paper blotted by little inky fingers, one might think it worth while to make the effort. But the effort would have to be great; a vast inertia would have to be overcome in order to effect an international agreement for uniform, simultaneous action. Nothing else would do. The Turks can do that (they did it), because they are only Turks. But we, Americans and English, can't; and, if we could, the Irish wouldn't. They'd demand free spelling and die for it.

.   .   .   .

We grown-up people are so habituated to our crazy alphabet that we do not realize the full enormity of its imperfection. When we learn that a Chinaman must retain a recollection of five thousand distinct picture-

form-combinations before he can do advanced reading, we are divided between amazement and pity. In
reality we are doing much the same thing. We have,
for instance, to learn the thirteen different ways of
indicating, by our spelling, the sound of long *o*—the
simplest, the earliest, and the last of all our utterances.
We must choose as among the following competitive
methods represented by the rival words: *note, boat,
toe, yeoman, soul, row, sew, hautboy, beau, owe, floor,
oh, O,"*—Very fittingly the list ends in *oh, O!* Since
each of the thirteen words could have been spelt in
any of twelve other ways, the list alone involves 169
choices. When we add to it all the other words that
have a long *o* sound, the choices will run into thousands, and the educated persons must remember by
sight every one of them. Conversely we have to remember by sight the varying pronunciations attached
to the combination *ough,* a thing which a Chinaman,
with only a few thousand pictures to recognize, thinks
atrocious.

These are not isolated vagaries, things of exception.
The confusion and effort involved run all through our
written language. What we are doing is in reality mem-
orizing a vast multitude of picture forms. The Chinaman sooner or later learns to read. So do we. We can
appreciate his ghastly loss of time. When we learn to
spell we are too young to understand about our own
till the thing is done.

The trouble is all with the instrument—our
wretched alphabet made worse by our use of it, a de-
terioration spread over centuries that multiplied its

original faults by thousands. The European peoples got lost in the maze of their own phonetics—so many rival forms, so many duplicate ways, so many alternate choices that spelling came to depend, as Mr. Weller said, on the taste and fancy of the speller.

When the explorers of America tried to write down in European spelling the Indian name now admitted to be Chicago, they wrote it in no less than twenty-one different fashions. Among these first prize may be awarded to *Stktschagto,* with honorable mention for *Tschakko*. A Chinaman starting with the Indian meaning of the word and not the sound would have made a little picture of a skunk, and scored one. Yet the alphabet, in its prime, was one of the great triumphs of the human race. It took its place beside the wheelbarrow, the dug-out canoe, and the iron pot, the stone ax and the great achievements that foreshadowed rotary motion, navigation, rum and conquest, and carried civilization round the world.

The other inventions went on. The wheelbarrow is an aeroplane and the dug-out a *Queen Mary*. The alphabet lagged behind. Its youth was its brightest period; the signs and the sounds probably fitted far better for the Phoenicians than for us. Our alphabet got into trouble. As it moved west and north it ran into new sounds and had no signs for them. The northern barbarians had a sound that we mark *th* which they got perhaps from the whistle of the wind at sea. Perhaps also they didn't. They had no sign for it, so they marked it with a *t* and an *h,* neither of which had anything to do with it, which perplexes still today the nascent minds of ten million children. The Greeks had a sign something like *th*, which probably sounded as something else, and that made further confusion.

Other letters crowded in, not needed. *Q*, with *u* always in attendance, stole the whole business that it gets from the letter *k*. The letter *c*, a mere cuckoo in the nest, took right and left from both *k* and *s*. In retaliation *x* crashed in as a sort of abbreviation that turned into a letter and fairly put *k* out of business, except that *x* couldn't start anything. *W* arose as a letter of despair: few people have a good enough sound-sense to hear what it really is. *P* and *h* joined in an illicit combination to steal from *f*—so that nowadays such words as *filosofy* look funny, nearly as funny as *funny* itself would if we spelt it *phunny*.

In other words our alphabet is a wreck. We could reform it easily enough if we were all of like mind and wanted to—easily enough, that is to say, with a few years' effort traded for a millennium of ease. But it would have to be done internationally, by authority, with finality and at a stroke. As it is, the way is blocked partly by the cranks in the foreground, but more by inertia in the background. Here for instance is the crank who explains that the gradations of vowel sounds are infinite and that no phonetic representation of them is possible except with an alphabet or system of infinite complexity. Of course the gradations are infinite. But so are the colours that run across the spectrum; yet we talk of a blue hat and a green light without any trouble. Anyone with an ear and tongue for linguistic phonetics can shade the broad sound of the letter *a* all the way from the parent called "father" at Oxford to the one called "fether" in Inverness. But a phonetic alphabet hits at a middle average which the individual varies at will in reading.

More pretentious is the scholarly crank who complains that phonetic spelling would hide the etymology of our language and draw a veil over its history. He likes the *b* in the word *debt* to carry him back to the dear old Latin *debitum*. He would rather sing a *psalm* in good company, than a *sam* with the ignorant. A *fotograf*, so spelt, would rob him of the Greek *Photos*, light, and *grapho*, I write, and make a mystery of clarity itself. But these objections rest on little more than the pang of novelty. We should all get as used to it in no time as we do to false teeth. In any case if one wants to play at scholarship and make a row over it, our spelling very often misleads, and hides the real origin of the word. Who put the false *u* in *honour* and the mistaken *s* in *island?* If the *g* in *reign* cheers us up by reminding us of *rego*, the *g* in *sovereign*, a false analogy, lets us down again. But all of this can be left for the scholars of the future to use in making theses.

A far more dangerous opponent is the advocate of "gradual spelling reform," who spoils a cause by accepting half of it, as if one should advocate being half drunk as a remedy for intemperance. He would have a thousand enthusiasts bind themselves together with a pledge to spell *cat* with a *k*. He lacks the visual imagination to see what a hopeless confusion gradual reform would introduce. It would be mending a coat of many colours with pieces from a patchwork quilt.

The only possible mode of introducing a new spelling of our common English and American language is by international agreement, authoritative and final, and done, after the ground is duly prepared and the method accepted, at a single stroke. Given ink enough and authority enough, we could do it in a year.

It would mean, it might be said, scrapping our present books. But we do that anyway. Few people, outside of college, read books more than five years old. All that are worth reading—the Macaulays and the Emersons, the Dickenses and the Mark Twains—would be re-spelt and re-printed. As for journalism, even as it is, last week's paper looks like ancient history. The newspapers could change their type as easily as they do their politics; and the machinery, as with politics, wouldn't need to change at all.

But it's no use. The dead weight of inertia puts it out of court. The change will only come as a side effect of some great issue which we cannot foresee. It took a whole world war to introduce "daylight-saving time," a thing advocated for two generations and as obvious as daylight itself.

．　　　．　　　．　　　．　　　˗　　　．　　　．

Our crazy spelling is at least free from one of the greater obstructions on the road to Parnassus. Each child learns to spell for himself. He is not held back to join a convoy of others for a joint attack on the letter *q*. And as soon as he can spell and read, the magic world of books, the enchantment of stories, the fascination of the past, are all open to him. This, in the world in which we live—a world of Sunday feature papers and cheap reprints and public libraries—has become the heritage of all. We are not like the pioneers who treasured in their log cabins a few tattered volumes, and whose children never saw a children's book.

And at this point education for oneself branches off from the beaten path of compulsory school. Arrived at this point a person of sufficient energy and individuality has power to educate himself. Even a university, as Carlyle or somebody said, is only a set of books. With sufficient interest and sufficient insight, a reasonable modicum of time free from work, and such advice as one can gather by the way, the path is open. But for the generality of people the path, though open, is too steep. Such overtime training of the mind, such individual effort and foresight are not for all. Yet, even for the laziest and the least gifted, at this point some measure of individual interest and urge must supplement the school and college curriculum. If not, the rest is vain.

But whether or not the average youthful scholar reads and studies for himself, he still belongs in the great convoy that moves forward year by year and class by class, in a measured phalanx of credits and units, its ranks checked into alignment by the current drill of examinations. It is difficult to see how it can be otherwise—for the education of the mass of the nation. We cannot afford a tutor for every child, and in any case you cannot feed with a spoon forever. But a realization of the tedium and delay of class education and of the false perspective given by examinations and credits will at least serve as a beginning for better things.

Class and credit work makes for overslowness by the very attempt to be "thorough," to cover every bit of ground before moving on to the next. This attitude toward education, though the students don't know it, comes to them as a legacy from the Jesuits in the opening period of modern education. Their maxim and practice of absolute thoroughness, the building in of every brick so that the wall shall never fall, was and is excellent within its scope; that is, when all else is disregarded—time and preference and individuality. It has in it all the grim infallibility of a machine.

In this it contrasts with the spontaneity of natural self-education, which stumbles eagerly forward, spells badly, but drives on to the hard words with the easy ones only half learned; pushes its elementary arithmetic on toward fractions with a shaky multiplication table bending under its feet like a trestle bridge over a canyon; picks up its history as a hen pecks for grain, its literature for the love of it, its art for art's sake.

It is the difference between a spirit and a mechanism, a substance and a shadow. And in the long run there is no education worth while, none with any meaning, except what we give ourselves or at least make our own. All that the best college can do is to offer opportunity and inspiration. I remember a bygone colleague of mine, a teacher of literature, who used to say to his class every year (professors always say everything once a year) : "Gentlemen, I spread the banquet. You

can take it or leave it as you like." The banquet was
his notes on *Comparative Literature* and looked a
pretty lean diet, but at least the idea was sound.

All that is best in what we call the liberal arts—
all the flowers of poetry and drama, literature and
history, imagination and inspiration—becomes distorted and disturbed by the system of examinations
and credits which deflect it from its proper semblance,
like the comic face seen in a convex mirror. Literature
looks in the mirror and reflects back as a "credit"—
a comic credit with a wide grinning mouth, hair stuck
out sideways and a brain-pan down to an inch and
a half. But this Credit is the real master for the student, controlling degrees, the entry to professions, jobs
—all that he came to college for. No wonder the figure
is grim—the joke on literature is so rich. The fellow
is like those malicious evil spirits that carry on our
humour in the next world, as malevolent buffoonery.
He says to the student, "Divide the beauty of poetry
into six elements and say them over to me, and I'll
give you a degree as a horse-doctor." Or he says,
"Name the six excellences of Shakespeare that your
professor told you out of his notes last October!"—
and he roars with laughter. "If you can't," he says,
"I won't let you out of college; you'll just stay shut
up there till you do. No law for you!"

The key to salvation is found by admitting once and
for all that a large part of knowledge cannot be tested
by written examinations, except to its own harm.
Things that are matters of appreciation, of feeling,
of taste, can be discussed, encouraged—fostered like

a plant in the sunlight of good teaching and interesting reading. But turn them into examinations and you defeat your own end.

I would make the school and college program consist of a maximum of stimulation and a minimum of examinations. Reading aloud, discussion, encouragement—something to kindle a flame, to light a lamp, to give the opportunity and the desire to read more. That is all that school can accomplish. To do this no great time is needed—not fifty per cent of what we give now—but more reality of purpose; in other words, not more quantity in the current of words, but a higher voltage in mental interest.

If I say that I would "shorten English literature" it is not because I would disparage a subject that has been for many years my life and livelihood. What I mean is that our teaching it is largely an attempt to teach the unteachable, to substitute text knowledge for literary appreciation, and the question-and-answer of a written examination for that "reading-for-reading's-sake" which is the only literary training worth talking about.

It is difficult to make one's meaning clear without slight or disparagement toward the thousands of earnest teachers giving excellent lessons and lectures on English literature. But their efforts are distorted out of their proper meaning by being set in a frame of "exams," "promotions," "matriculations," "degrees" and entrances to the "professions." That is enough to poison the love of literature at the root.

The teaching of literature should mean, at the beginning, reading of worth-while books to little children who can't read. Without false sentiment, it may be said that most people carry as their chief literary asset the remembrance of "What mother read aloud to them when they were kids." But then "mother" never held exams, or asked the children to name the six chief beauties of Robinson Crusoe, or to give parallel passages to Old Mother Hubbard and the Snow Queen. The reading was for reading's sake, and it led the child into the magic garden to which presently, able to read, he could resort of himself; out of the garden the school-teacher afterwards chased him with a written exam.

This is the fact of the matter. There is a certain utility and a certain scope for written examinations. But there is ground upon which the written examination cannot touch without withering all that grows on it. At the beginning of learning, for the sake of its later love and enjoyment, there are certain things that must be committed to memory. These things are not so much education as the frame in which education is set. Children must learn the multiplication table. Medical students must learn the names of the three hundred odd bones of the human body. Not that the names in themselves are anything. But they are necessary for familiar reference. One recalls the enthusiastic young lady who said that the astronomers must be wonderfully clever to have found out the names of the stars. A medical man must be at least as wonderful as that; and any kind of examination, any "yes"-and-"no" test is in order so as to see if he really is. So, in history, examination is in order on lists of the dates of kings and of battles. These are not history but are the necessary pegs on which to hang it. The historical knowledge of many people is badly damaged by not remembering whether the French Revolution or the American Revolution came first, and just where Peter the Great came in and whether he was Peter the Hermit.

It is the fashion today to discredit kings even as pegs. We are told to think of history as the movement of peoples; but it's hard to peg history on that: "movement No. 1," "movement No. 2," "fine movement about 1066," and so on. The older method of treating the death of Queen Anne as a landmark is far better. But of course when all that is done and learned, real history is yet to begin.

So with literature. It is proper no doubt for pupils and even college students to answer questions— straight "yes"-and-"no" as to who lived when and who wrote what. But the moment you go further and give examination questions of the six chief beauties of Wordsworth, and the six chief sillinesses of Milton, education has run to a dead end. Much of liberal arts in the best sense is not ground for written examination. We must alter the curriculum so that a lot of it is only for students who want it. The practical difficulty is obvious; since mere attendance, and perhaps not even that, would be needed for a credit. But at least students could be encouraged to *write,* not on examinations, but on what they thought about what they read; and their work could be estimated from that.

But the main contention is that education in literature must, after its first initiation, be self-prompted, that is must depend on individual appreciation, or it is no good. If it stops with college it should never have begun. It should grow into the student's life till it becomes part of it and remains with him till old age, the period in which people no longer read, but re-read what they have loved before.

Contrast with the dilemma thus offered, as between spontaneous interest and mechanical drill, the fortunate position of history. Here is a subject which by happy circumstance is coming into its own. The moving picture has proved a fairy godmother, giving to each of us a magic mirror to replace the dusty pages. . . . Look! Here comes Charlemagne; notice how he is dressed, see the queer twisted suit of iron made of little chains! . . . and the way the men wear their hair on their shoulders and their long pointed spears! And here's Henry VIII; of course you recognize him; he was here last year as Charles Laughton. Funny breeches they used to wear, eh? . . . And so we sit under the enchantment of half darkness, and before us a magic scroll unfolds and the dead voices speak, and all the pageant of the past rolls down before us. Here, indeed, is America discovered! See the Spanish caravels tossing on the waves and the huge banners all purple, crimson and gold . . . and so on downward. We are comrades in arms with Washington . . . we refight the battle of New Orleans . . . and, far out on the plains among the painted Shawnees and Cheyennes, we drive the last golden spike of the railways that unite a continent.

No such page in education was ever turned. It shows what all education might be, if desire and opportunity ran thus together. It has its dangers. One might have thought that the picture people would be too careless of fact, too much like the Shakespearean "producer" who would put up a board and mark it *Athens*. There was indeed such a tendency at first. In a first picture of the battle of New Orleans of 1815, so I have been told, an electric street car moved sedately through a British regiment. And I have it on the authority of Mr. Irvin Cobb that an early New England village scene of the Revolutionary War had a huge street sign in it: *Joe's Garage, Gasoline at All Hours.*

But the tendency turned the other way. It seemed that the public revelled in the new accuracy of history. They liked to see Charlemagne's hair and Napoleon's coat just as they were and watch Talleyrand take snuff out of the very kind of box that Talleyrand used to take snuff out of. And the moving picture people, good fellows, asked nothing better than to give the people what the people wanted and gave it to them.

Historians whose turn for accuracy exceeds their limit of tolerance have it the other way and tell us that the moving pictures are distorting history. One of Harvard's best tells us, for example, that "the clownish posturing of film heroes has obscured the authentic American cowboy." It may be so—a little. But the historian must realize that there must be a little distortion in all art; the colours must be a little heightened to make the object visible. Dante had to make hell a little more spiral than it really is; all heroines must be too beautiful and all heroes a little overbrave.

The moving picture, so far, has not sinned beyond the legitimate exaggeration of romantic art. What it will do next, we don't know, except that it will give the people what the people want. If they tire of accuracy and want Charlemagne to be a little more comic and wear a tuxedo; or if, as is likely, they presently want the epochs mixed up, so as to have Abraham Lincoln and Julius Caesar in the same film, they'll get that also.

Meantime history has fallen heir to a wonderful legacy, to treasure or to squander. All the world is back at school, as it ought to be, for school in the proper sense should last a lifetime. People who had "finished" history at high school are taking it up again in the dark, at fifty cents per epoch.

·   ·   ·   ·   ·   ·   ·

Natural science is almost as happily situated as history. There is no doubt about its place in the curriculum and no difficulty in awarding it. Every educated person needs a "thorough smattering" of science, a little piece off the top, so to speak; and no one but a specialist can hope for more. The time for that is gone. The last man who knew everything died about the time of Professor Huxley. As was said in an earlier chapter, the learned men of the Middle Ages "knew it all." The scholars of the Renaissance knew it all and asked for more. The professors of the nineteenth century knew it all and could just hold it. In the twentieth, it ran over at the top.

At the present day the educated man must be content with that "outline" of science which gives us the cream without our aspiring to milk the cow. The prevalence of popular "outlines," "digests" and "abstracts" is evidence of a world seeking nature's remedy for the overcrowding of the human mind.

But science is peculiar in that the top is the best of it, like the rose which crowns the thorns or the South Sea island that rises in beauty from the laborious coral below. I know no better hours than those that take flight into the majestic distances of astronomy, the mysteries of four-dimensional space-time and the vast atom filled with agitated nothingness. "A tale, told by a scientist, full of sound and fury and signifying nothing." Here science fades away to mysticism, and knowledge reverts to its second childhood and dies as ignorant as at its birth.

In natural science—I like the old-fashioned term, no doubt quite indefensible—I include, first, physics. This in its plain sense of motion and force, mass and momentum, can be taught without mysticism and without reference to the later difficulties as to where is here, and when is now, and what is action at a distance. This newer perplexity is not needed for the study of phenomena. I understand that the old-time physics of absolute space and time breaks if you stretch it far enough. Light, it seems, gets whisked round the edge of a planet like a hat blown round a windy corner. Isaac Newton didn't know this, but students can still dream it off for a century or two and still take their physics straight. It is better for a pupil to learn physics without afterthought as to absolute space and time, just as it is better for a child always to think of its parents as happily married, and not learn the truth till later.

This program of physics can be tucked in under mathematics and used as material to make the kind of legitimate problems to which I referred above. It can serve, so to speak, as the handy man of mathematics.

Where physics branches off into the wave-world— electricity, light, radio, and cosmic emanations—a special teaching is necessary. But in this the ordinary student can never go far. The investigation is too vast. Yet a year of school and a year of college should keep him from the ignorance that was, and should make of him and his fellows a sort of seed-bed, a plot of selection, from which are chosen the real scholars and physical scientists to whom we entrust our guidance in the knowledge needed for our life and for the death of our enemies.

The ancient science of the rock is simple in its outline, but it makes no demand on the curriculum that is not amply justified and it carries with it as yet no fool appendages that need curtailing. The science of life—the whole "biology"—fills a larger field. But it can be cut loose from the additions that make it appear larger than it is, from the "bogus" attempts to make science where none is—as with the unsurveyed empire staked out by sociology, and the bottomless mine put on the market by psychology. Apart from these things, the outline of biological science, vital as it is, puts no undue strain on education.

In the matter of physiology, the knowledge of the human body (for people who are never to be students of medicine), I think I would go slow. I would be inclined to leave it out altogether. This is a heretical opinion, no doubt, and very different from the dogma, current since Huxley, that the wise child must know its own body. I doubt whether it is good for society that the ordinary plain man should know much of the details of how his body works. The man who has learned to think of his heart as a pump, with an intake in it as valves that get out of order, is on the way toward having a weak one. Better let him think of it as the seat of love and generosity, and it will beat away happily till it stops. Let him think of his stomach as where he puts his dinner, not as a fierce chemical furnace where acids are tearing up tissues and sending up exhaust gases like the back end of a tannery. Let him think of his bowels as the bowels of compassion, as gentle as the New Testament, and his blood as part of his lineage, not as the battleground of a myriad of good and evil corpuscles, some on his side and some dead set against him. Any man who has realized that he has in him about twenty-five feet of colon and semicolon—a sort of string of sausages—can never think the same of himself again.

These little scraps of knowledge, you see, are of no practical use, and the mental effect of them is to turn the man, in his own eyes, from the vague image of God that he was to the dirty contraption full of mess that one year's physiology makes of him. There he sits on his bench in the doctor's consulting room, full of rumblings and inward visions. Cure him? You can't. That's just the trouble. Ask any of your medical friends. The man is all in the wrong frame of mind to be cured. To cure him you have to revert to that image of God which, to higher vision, turns out to be true after all, and which heals an ailment with a thought. This man can't. He knows too much, or too little. His first-year physiology sends him to his death when a peasant or a sailor or a child, being still an image of God, would go on living.

It is easy for a student, as for anybody else, to learn the few simple laws of health—to come in out of the wet, not to eat more than he can pay for, to wear a hat in the sun and to sleep with his window open and his mouth shut. Public health, also—if you like, teach that in college, even to ordinary students. That sewers stink, phew! that mosquitos carry yellow fever; that people died of the Great Plague because of dirt, and that everybody needs fresh air every minute, indoors and out—all of this you can study and feel all the brighter and more wholesome for knowing it. But this, or as much of this as educated people need, a student, apart from a medical student, can learn in a few afternoon lectures as a listener-in, and stay convinced and be a clean, well-ventilated citizen ever afterward.

For physiology at large—as for certain other things that masquerade as sex-education and which I leave out of this book as not fit to go into it—I put in a plea for a snug corner of ignorance. But the topic is too large to treat here, and I leave it for a later opportunity.

III

What Good Is Latin?

CHAPTER III

WHAT GOOD IS LATIN?

The vitamins of education — Latin the mainstay of the technical study of language — Latin as ballast — Greek only for philologists and Apostles — Latin composition for business correspondence — Mediaeval versus stream-lined Latin — You can't read Latin? Neither could the Romans

OUR medical people of today talk much of vitamins. Just what they are I do not know, but they are sub-divided and named, with the rich imaginative fancy of the scientist, Vitamin A, Vitamin B, and so on as dis-covered. These I understand enter into our diet and have a peculiar importance in it. If we are misguided enough to stop eating any one of these vitamins, it is all over with us. When I first learned this, I was in-clined, if only for precaution's sake, to give up bacon and eggs and roast beef and adopt an exclusive diet of vitamins as everywhere freely advertised at a price equal merely to what we have got. But I have since been told by an eminent medical authority that it would be very hard for an ordinary human being, fed in the ordinary way, to avoid eating all the vitamins that there are; in fact, he can't help eating them. The good they do is so universal and so unobtrusive that for thousands of years it was never analyzed and specified.

Now, I regard Latin as one of the vitamins of education. If mathematics is Vitamin A, and reading and writing is Vitamin B, Latin can certainly get in somewhere not far down the alphabet. The study of Latin has in two thousand years so worked itself into the living tissue of our education that we only realize on reflection the peculiar part it plays. It gives us our first real consciousness of what language is. We discover that language is not, as it must seem to savages, "inevitable." After its first twilight beginnings in onomatopoeia and muscular grunts, it becomes a mere convention between sound and significance. Readers of Mark Twain will recall how Huck Finn and Nigger Jim fell into a linguistic discussion as to whether or not it was believable that a Frenchman didn't call a cow a "cow." Jim easily proved to Huck that, if he *knew* it was a cow he'd have to call it so. The humour of the passage rests on the missing postulate as to what language is. Unconsciously students of elementary Latin acquire this new detachment from words. With it they begin to change from the servants to the masters of language. They can reset, remake it, and turn it to new use.

And here in the technical study of language, with a view to improving our mastery of our own, I find Latin of incomparable utility. It is sufficiently near and yet sufficiently far from our own idiom to turn translation into an art, involving a nice sense of language meaning and a nice ingenuity in handling language forms. To translate back and forward two kindred modern languages is of little linguistic value. It only occasionally involves translation in the higher sense. It is simply mere substitution. On the other hand, as between our languages and an agglutinative Asiatic speech, like Japanese, the distance is too great for the form of exercise of which I speak. I remember years and years ago in teaching elementary French in school asking a pupil how you say in French, "Give me some bread." He answered, "You can't say it; you have to say something else." So it is with Japanese; you must get the idea, start over again, and "say something else."

But with Latin the translator finds a phrase—let us take a simple one such as *"Quae cum ita sint,"* of which the meaning is clear and the single words ridiculous—for our use. He beats about the bush until he finds at quite a distance in a different thicket such a phrase as "This being the case." Anyone not capable of a glow of intellectual pleasure at such an achievement is not fit to study language.

Words, of course, are nothing as beside things. The philologist and the grammarian seem to their active brethren to be groping among the dead. Yet even for them there must be moments of exultation, of despair, of triumph—as of Browning's dying grammarian who settled "the enclitic *De,* dead from the waist down." And I think, too, of the wonderful work of King James' translators, balanced between literalism and innovation, and often conveying truth at its best when furthest from it in substance. Consider the verse, as it was written in the Greek, "O Death, where is thy sting, O Hades, where is thy victory?" Literal translation becomes either irreverent or comic. But how wonderful

when they wrote, "O Death, where is thy sting, C
Grave, thy victory?"

.   .   .   .

So much for the value of Latin as a mainstay for
the technical study of language. But, to my thinking, a
further reason for retaining it as the base of our edu
cation is because it can serve, so to speak, as ballast
It is the ballast in the hold of a ship, down in the dark
and unseen, which governs every graceful dip and dive
of the flag at the masthead and guarantees against
disaster. Or we may take another metaphor from one
of those odd little mantelpiece figures of mandarins o.
patriarchs whose nodding head rocks back and for
ward but never falls because of a controlling ball o
lead suspended in his belly. For those of us trained in
a classical education Latin is the ball of lead in ou:
bellies which keeps our eyes properly focused on the
horizon.

What I mean is this. We are in danger now, in ou
rushing mechanical world, of rearing a generation with
no backward outlook, living in two dimensions only
without thought of the past. For such people histor
only goes back as far as the last presidential election
with dim figures such as Grover Cleveland and Quee
Victoria as a sort of mythology. Yet for all wise think
ing, for all careful social control, it is necessary to se
things as they have grown, to look on our institution
in the light of their past. Such dim vision as we ca
have of the future depends absolutely on this. Cut of
the human race from the knowledge and comprehen
sion of its history, and its government will just tur

nto a monkey cage. We need the guidance of history.
All our yesterdays it is true have only lighted fools the
way to dusty death. But we need at least the dates of
he yesterdays and the list of the fools.

Now a great deal of our necessary education of
oday consists of matter that has nothing to do with
he past. Mathematics is eternal. Astronomy runs eternity a close second. Physics—dynamics, electricity and
all that—is as instantaneous as a flash of lightning.
These things are taught as existing simply "here" and
"now"; and even "here" and "now," since Einstein,
must hurry up to get over. Other subjects there are
which are certainly historical and old but fail to serve
he purpose of a balanced outlook. Geology is old, but
t is *too* old. Not even an English conservative can take
a geological view of politics. Even the most cautious
must move a little faster than palaeontology.

But ballast there must be. If the "instantaneous"
subjects are left alone, the world of an intelligent
school-boy becomes all *present* and no past, a huge
shop window with no depth to it. One recalls the story
of the man who knew himself to be addicted to boast-
ing and exaggeration and used therefore to check himself suddenly and correct his statement. "My green-
house," he said, "is twenty feet high and a hundred
feet long"; then he paused and added, "but it's only a
foot wide." Such in aspect would be the kind of razzle-
dazzle world of scarcely more than two dimensions
that our practical and scientific education must tend to
make. The other dimension that must be added to it,
he ballast that must give it stability, is found in the

historical subjects and in Latin, as a sort of open door
leading into the great world of the past. Even the dullest draws his lesson from the millennium of its history

It could be desired that every subject could be taught
historically. The student might learn his mathematics
from the counting of fingers and toes, that gave us our
repeating ten, and our "score"; the "abacus" and the
"counter" of the mediaeval shop; the Hindu-Arabian
decimal system; Napier's bones and Descartes' co-
ordinates and Newton's calculus. Still better, if physics
could be learned step by step and stage by stage as it
was disclosed by the great minds that revealed it; and
so with all the rest. Thus would the individual mind
repeat the intellectual evolution of the race, as the individual body does from embryo to adult. But time
forbids. *Ars longa.*

Yet within a possible degree the same effect on outlook may be produced by ballasting our education with
the past world and with Latin as its representative
tongue. For Greek I hold no brief. It is only for philologists and Apostles. It can no longer be a part of
the education of every college man. Professors tell us
that Greek literature is vastly superior to Latin. It
may well be, without hurting itself, since Latin literature, apart from its setting in history, amounts to very
little. It is claimed that Greek philosophy and the
Greek drama are superior to modern. There is no way
to disprove this. People who have never learned Greek
are outside of the discussion. Those of us who learned
Greek and dissent from it are ruled out of the argument. The dead judgment of authority rules. Person

ally I only know one department of literature in which I feel the full right to an opinion; that of the literature of humour. To my mind the wit of Aristophanes is about as funny as the jokes of a village cut-up. To name him in the class with people like Charles Dickens and Mark Twain and A. P. Herbert and Bob Benchley and myself is just nonsense. This statement is absolute and without appeal.

But for the rest of Greek literature, let it pass. The world has no time for it, excepting only those, the fortunate few, who go to college and stay there for ever, whose happy lot I eulogize in the concluding chapter. For them, the real scholars, trustees of the world's heritage of learning, let there be Greek. For them the six cases, and the three numbers—you, and you two, and you all—and all the moods and voices and tenses that fill a book as large as Goodwin's so full that no student ever sees the last page. For that, and for our heritage of the New Testament, Greek must stay. But for the ordinary scholar, none of it. You can't learn a little Greek; it won't divide; it's like a billiard ball. Half of it is no good.

.   .   .   .

But even taking Latin on the terms of the plain business man, who wants to see the dollars and cents in everything, there is a great deal to be said for it. I know no better asset for a young man entering business life than the ability to express himself well in speech and in writing. Anyone with enough of this ability and training need never wonder where to find a living. Not everybody can be a literary genius or an orator. But everybody can learn to speak and to write to the full extent of his natural endowment, just as everybody can learn to swim, and nobody can swim without learning. A course in Latin is about the best training in this direction. Boys learn to write good English sentences by writing bad Latin ones. The notion that there is a special technical language for use in business correspondence is a myth sedulously fostered by commercial colleges. Technical business language consists of a few such things, as "F.O.B.," "ex-dividend," "your Mr. Smith," "our Miss McCarthy," "yours of the third ult. received and would say," etc., etc. A Latin student could learn it all on one page. As for writing, so for speech. Practice and opportunity are needed, but the basis is words. Salesmanship, or the art of over-persuasion, can be learned as Latin prose composition.

. . . .

But granting that we are to teach Latin in the schools and colleges and make it in a way the bedrock basis of linguistic study, we have to try to get rid of some of the dead weight that has carried down the ages. Latin comes to us from earlier days when it was the one great study, the very ground on which education stood. So it was taught, as they did everything in the Middle Ages, regardless of time and with one eye on eternity. In the Middle Ages when they built a wall they built it as for five hundred years to come; and when they taught Latin, they did it in the same way, with the foundations laid away down below ground, and "underpinned," like the wall of a cathedral resting on a bed of white oak.

That is to say, in the schools of the past, when they taught the third declension, they taught it all; not the genitive and the gender of *some* of the nouns but the genitive and the gender of *all* of the nouns. There is something absolute and admirable in the very completeness of it. They did it with infinite repetition and with little rhymes and tags, what they called *memoria technica*, such as:

> *Substantives in do and go*
> *Genus femininum show;*
> *But ligo, ordo, praedo, cardo,*
> *Are masculine, and common margo.*

Such a system was all right for the people of the age. It took an infinity of time, but there was little else to learn.

People who underwent the same kind of training as I had fifty years ago learned their Latin on this mediaeval system. They came away from it with the impression that they had nearly reached the promised land but failed to get there, shipwrecked in sight of port. A little more and we would have "known Latin." As it is, we only carry with us still a lot of little tags and lists from which the meaning has gone but which still keep their outline like the gossamer skeleton of a dead dragon-fly.

> *A, ab, and absque, cum, coram, de,*
> *E or ex, prae, pro, tenus, sine—*

What about them? I don't know.
Dic, duc, fac, fur—what's wrong with them? Some-

thing crooked there, I'm sure, but I forget it.

Now I think I could get all the result we want as mental and literary training and cut out at least fifty per cent of Latin instruction. I would teach Latin grammar in a plain way with very little attention to oddities and exceptions. Let the pupils live and die without knowing that *bobus* can also be written as *bubus;* that the Latin for "liver" is irregular and the verb "I drink" is peculiar in the past. Let them wait a while to learn that the dative plural of *dea* is *deabus;* wait till they meet goddesses in actual life. People taught in this way will be reading Caesar almost as soon as they begin the language and writing plain Latin sentences as regular as a Roman wall.

I say that I think that I could get all the cultural result needed and cut out fifty per cent of the time taken. But I admit there's a certain doubt about it; my friends who are today professors and teachers of Latin tell me that the antiquated system of which I speak has quite gone out. It has been superseded by newer methods which some of them like to call "stream-lined" Latin. The phrase is typical of our day; we all move in the mass, holding one idea at a time. Because the aeroplane had to be "stream-lined," on account of its excessive speed, we stream-line everything, down to a hearse. The metaphor spreads like a ripple in a pond. A professor teaches stream-lined Latin to a class of stream-lined girls. But let the phrase pass and take it for what it means, Latin learned quickly.

Now in the first place I don't believe there's as much

stream-lining in the schools as its chief advocates believe. There are many teachers who by instinct value an exception more than a rule. Hide the exceptions at the back of the grammar, after the index, and they'll find them as a cow finds water. So with the examiners; they lived on a diet of exceptions too long to swear off. You never know when they may break out into irregularities. Better learn them.

In the second place stream-lining is apt to go so far that there's nothing left. You get the pupil so flattened out that he has become caseless, voiceless, tenseless, and moodless. For him there is no joy in the ethical dative or the genitive of value or the accusative of nearer definition. They're all one to him. He may be all right in an aeroplane because there's no friction left in him. But his "Latin" has just turned into a bunch of "roots," like the language of pigeon Chinese, or Pottawatamie English. When a Chinaman speaking "pigeon" (that is, *business* language) wishes to indicate the Episcopal Bishop of Hong Kong he calls him the "A.I. top-side, Heaven-pigeon man." That is exactly how Latin must look to the stream-lined student, just a collection of chunks of language to be sorted out for significance.

Nor does ready-made translation help. If we read Pliny in English and Virgil in prose, that's English not Latin. But never mind. There must be some way of compromise, to set us free from the dilemma, that steers between the Scylla of too much and the Charybdis of too little. The problem is to preserve enough of the old rigid discipline of moods and tenses, rules and exceptions to strengthen the mind without arresting it.

.　　.　　.　　.　　.　　.

I revert again in conclusion to the objection that so many of us might make that we learnt Latin for years in school and college and never got anywhere with it, never got to be able to read it straight off. Of course we didn't. Nobody ever does. Not even the professors; no, nor the Romans themselves, not in the way that we read English. This is of course a sort of official secret handed down for generations, and I am really violating here the obligation of my profession by divulging it. But perhaps the time has come to remove the veil. Hitherto it has been better for the world to pretend that at least somebody could "read Latin straight off." Now it is better to have the truth. The Romans themselves couldn't.

I am prepared to support this statement. Written language in Roman days, before printing and newspapers, was on a quite different footing from what it is now. There was the ordinary speech of ordinary people, jabbering away all day, just as we do now, with fragments of sentences, exclamations, phrases, false starts and short circuits. Except on the stage, conversation is never done out in full periods, unless by old maids, professors, and garrulous village philosophers; and done thus it is always either ludicrous or tiresome. But we moderns have a written language also of easy and rapid comprehension because we need it for the daily news and the love romances and the crime stories of which the Romans had no current supply. For them

one love story had to last a thousand years, from Dido
till the fall of Rome. So when they *wrote,* it was different. They took up the pen as a man puts on his Sunday
clothes; they were not trying to be easily intelligible.
They wanted to get the full effect, and expected it to
take a few moments' reflection to grasp it. I am quite
sure that if one read out an oration of Cicero to a
Roman who had never heard it he would soon get
mixed and interrupt to say, "Read that last paragraph
again, will you?" Just as you yourself would do, if
someone read you a section of Browning without fair
warning. The parallel is exact. Browning and Cicero
were doing the same thing, proposing to sacrifice immediate comprehension for the sake of deeper comprehension when comprehended.

But, you say, some of Cicero's writings were
speeches made in court? Not at all; in court they
didn't sound like that, and they were retouched afterwards. A glance at the pages of the *Congressional
Record* will show what is meant.

I remember once when I was a master at school giving a prize of a cake, specially made, with all sorts
of icing and emblems—a joy to look at. The baker
showed it to me and received my congratulations with
obvious pleasure. But he was an honest man, and he
said, "I'm not saying, sir, that it will be much of a cake
for eating." I assured him that no one would think of
doing anything as brutal as that. So with the Roman
writings—not much of writings for understanding.

All this I say by way of comforting those who, like
myself, studied Latin for years and never were able
to read it—unless we had read it already.

IV

Mathematics Versus Puzzles

CHAPTER IV

MATHEMATICS VERSUS PUZZLES

Are mathematical judgments synthetically a priori —
The multiplication table a fair hand-to-hand fight —
Puzzles a fraud — Mr. Brown and the equation —
Mathematics and mystifications; Two gazinta four —
Can we improve our mathematical sense?

I REMEMBER being taken as a boy of twelve years old
to listen to a "paper" at the University of Toronto
Literary and Debating Society, on the question, "Are
mathematical judgments synthetically *a priori?*" In
those simple days before "pictures" and radio and
motor-cars and emancipated girls, to go and listen to
a "paper" or to a debate between two black-robed students, sipping water off a table, was presumed to be
first-class fun. When they discussed mathematical judgments and whether or not *a priori,* I felt that I didn't
understand it, but that I would when I grew up. That's
where I was wrong.

I am still very vague as to what mathematical judgments being synthetically *a priori* means. I imagine it
refers to the question how do we know that one and
one makes two, and if it does, what do we mean by it?
But at any rate it bears witness to the profundity of
mathematics—I mean, its reach toward the infinite
and the unknowable.

This element of fundamental mystery has been expanded in our own day by the glorious confusion introduced by Professor Einstein into all our notions of distance, time and magnitude. How far is one thing from another? The question becomes unknowable. It may be twice as far away as something else is, or half as far; but, beyond the relative number, there seems no such thing as solid distance. What is a foot? Twelve inches. What is an inch? One twelfth of a foot. Similarly where is *here?* And when is *now?*

I only refer to these mysteries in order to explain why I still have to speak of mathematics in a reverential whisper, like a Christian entering a Mohammedan mosque, in wicker slippers. He knows it's a reverend place though he doesn't understand it.

My attitude toward mathematics, indeed, is that of nine out of ten of educated people—a sense of awe, something like horror, a gratitude for escape but at times a wistful feeling of regret, a sense that there might have been more made of it. Everything, therefore, that I say about mathematics is tempered by so great a humility as to rob it of all controversial aspect. But I do think that as far as a practical school curriculum goes I could shorten it by at least one half. What I would do, to express it in a single phrase, would be to separate true mathematics from mathematical puzzles.

If mathematics is for many students the dragon in the path, these puzzles are the dragon's teeth. Take them out and the dragon is as easy to handle as a cow. Children learn to count and add and multiply, and feel that it is all plain and straightforward; the multiplication table may be tricky, but it's fair. Then presently comes a "puzzle" problem. "What number," says the teacher to the child, "is made up of two figures, the second meaning twice as many as the first, and the two adding up to nine?"

Now, this is not mathematics in the proper sense; this is a puzzle. The only true mathematical operation here would be to set down all the numbers of two digits, from 10 to 99 in turn, and see which one fitted it. But when it comes to guessing and choosing, to ingenuity, that's a puzzle. Half our school mathematics in algebra and geometry consist of "puzzles," freak equations and inventive geometry. Students are not discoverers. Pythagoras solved the problem of the squares on the right-angled triangle. I'm willing to "take it as read" and learn it in ten minutes.

This puzzle "bunker" is built right across the mathematical fairway and down the middle of it. "Scholars" pound the sand in it and wonder why they can't do mathematics. True mathematics means a process learned and used; hard to learn, but later, second nature. Show me how to extract a square root and I'll extract it as neatly as a dentist. Tell a ship's captain how to calculate the angle of the sun's declination and show a broker's clerk how to use logarithms for compound interest. But don't expect a student to be a discoverer, working out "problems" which Isaac Newton or Copernicus might solve or miss.

Now at the present time all school-books on mathematics are mixtures of what may be called "sums," "problems" and "mathematical puzzles." A sum is an operation dealing with numbers and following a definite and known routine of calculation. When a waiter adds up a restaurant cheque he performs a sum. A calculating machine can do a sum. But it can't do a problem. For a problem is an operation involving a selection of methods of calculation, of which only certain ones will fit the case. A school-boy calculating when the hour hand of a clock will overtake the minute hand is working out a problem. There are plenty of wrong ways of working at it, as when Achilles tried to overtake a tortoise, and kept the Greeks guessing for generations. But the school-boy soon finds that there are a whole lot of problems dealing with motion and time which all fall into a definite and known method of solution that becomes itself as familiar as the waiter's addition table. Now the extension of a problem in difficulty and intricacy, to where only one method of many will bring a solution, turns it, at some point, into a puzzle.

When Archimedes jumped out of his bath and shouted "Eureka," what he had solved was not a problem but a puzzle. He had been asked by some king or other, had he not? how to tell whether a gold crown was really a gold crown or was made of two metals melted together. A modern chemist would find this out with an acid. But Archimedes found a way without chemistry. Yet a professor of mathematics might take a bath every morning for years and never think of it. Since there was no way of forcing a solution by an inevitable method, the thing was not a problem but a puzzle.

Such a puzzle is legitimate enough, though it is no true test of mathematical knowledge. But further out on the field are puzzles that may be called illegitimate, since they present the added difficulty of misleading or paradoxical language. For the information and perhaps the diversion of the reader, let me illustrate the difference. Here is a legitimate puzzle. A man wishes to buy a piece of linoleum that is to cover a space 12 feet by 12. A dealer offers him a piece that is 9 feet by 16 feet. Obviously each piece contains 144 square feet. The dealer tells the customer that all he needs to do is to cut the piece that is 9 feet by 16 feet into two separate pieces that can then be fitted together to cover 12 feet by 12 feet. This of course—or rather *not* of course, for few people can do it—is done by drawing lines across the 12 x 12 piece, 3 feet apart in one direction and 4 feet in the other. Start 9 feet east from the top north-west corner and cut along the lines alternately south and west, and there you are. But such a puzzle does not belong in mathematical education although it corresponds in nature to a lot of the things called "problems" that wreck the lives of students.

Here however is a sample of an illegitimate puzzle. A man has 17 camels. He leaves them in his will to his three sons, ½ to the eldest, ⅓ to the next and ⅑ to the youngest. But these fractions won't divide unless you cut up the camels themselves. When the sons are still in perplexity a Dervish happens to pass by, riding on a camel. Dervishes always ride by on camels at con-

venient moments in these Arabian problems. The sons
tell him of their dilemma. After deep thought—Dervishes always think deeply—he says, "Let me lend you
my camel to make eighteen instead of seventeen. Now
take one half which is nine, and one third which is six,
and one ninth which is two, and you each have your
proper share. And as *nine* and *six* and *two* only add
up to seventeen, you may kindly return my camel."
With which the Dervish departed, and the sons no
doubt told the story all the rest of their lives.

Now this problem is of course as full of fallacies as
a sieve is full of holes. In the first place the sons didn't
get one half and one third and one ninth of 17 but of
something else: and when the father left them these
fractions, a little arithmetic—beyond them, no doubt—
would have shown that ½ and ⅓ and ⅑ of a thing
don't add up to the whole thing but only to $^{17}\!/_{18}$ of it.
There was still $\frac{1}{18}$ of each camel coming to somebody.

Here is another type of puzzle problem turning on
misleading suggestion. Three men at a summer hotel
were going fishing and were told they must pay 10 dollars each for a license. They each put up 10 dollars
and sent it by a hotel-boy to the inspector's office. The
boy came back with 5 dollars and said that the inspector had made a rebate of 5 dollars out of 30, because it was understood they were all one party in the
same boat. The men, greatly pleased, gave the boy 2
dollars out of the 5 and kept one each. One of them
then said: "Look here! This is odd. We expected our
fishing to cost ten dollars each (thirty dollars) and it
has only cost us nine dollars each, and two to the boy.

Three times nine is twenty-seven, and two makes twenty-nine; where has the other dollar of the thirty gone?"

The reader no doubt sees the fallacy instantly; but some people wouldn't.

Now I admit that text-books on mathematics never push the problems quite as far as this on illegitimate puzzle ground—unless indeed they do it on purpose, as in the book of *Mathematical Recreations* once compiled by the celebrated Professor Ball. But what I claim is that the element of the problem, and even of the puzzle, looms far too large in mathematics as we have it. Indeed for most people it overshadows the subject and ends their advance.

The ordinary straight "discipline" of school mathematics should consist of plain methods of calculation, like division, square root, highest common factor and so on, or such problems as conform to a recognized method of regular solution. All that goes in arithmetic under the name of the "unitary method" is of this class. If A in one hour can do twice as much work as B does in two hours, then—well, we know all about them. Yet few people realize that this beautiful and logical unitary method is quite new—I mean belongs only in the last two generations. When I first learned arithmetic it was just emerging from the "rule-of-three" in the dim light of which all such calculations appeared something like puzzles.

In algebra also a vast part of the subject can be studied as regular calculation, or at least as a problem of regular order, such as the motion and time illustra-

tion mentioned above. I gather, also, that another
large section of algebraical calculation, though capable
of being effected by short, ingenious, or individual
methods, can always, if need be, be submitted to a
forced operation, clumsy but inevitable—as if a person
wanting to know how many squares there are on a
chess-board counted them one by one.

To illustrate what I mean, let me call back, from
nearly sixty years ago, the recollection of our Sixth
Form class in mathematics at Upper Canada College.
Our master, Mr. Brown, was a mathematician, the real
thing, with a gold medal in proof of it, and gold spec-
tacles through which he saw little but x and y—gentle,
simple and out of the world. The class had early dis-
covered that Mr. Brown, with a long equation on the
black-board and his back to the class, would stay there
indefinitely, in his academic cap and gown, lost in a
reverie in which the bonds of discipline fell apart. So
the thing was to supply him with a sufficiently tough
equation.

This became the special business of the *farceur* of
the class, a large and cheerful joker called Donald
Armour, later on the staff of the Rush Medical College and a distinguished Harley Street surgeon. Armour would approach Mr. Brown in the morning and
say: "I was looking over some Woolwich examination
papers last night, Mr. Brown, and I found this equation. I can't make anything of it." "Oh!" said Mr.
Brown with interest. He accepted without question the
idea that Armour spent his evenings in mathematics.
"Let me look at it, Armour." Then another spirit in

collusion would call out, "Won't you put it on the board, Mr. Brown?" And in a minute there it was, strung out along the black-board, a tangled mass of x's and y's and squares and cubes, with Mr. Brown in front of it, as still as Rodin's *penseur*.

Meanwhile the class relaxed into easy conversation, and Armour threw paper darts with pins in the end to try and hit Mr. Brown in the yoke of his gown. Presently, without turning round, Mr. Brown spoke. "Of course, I could *force* it . . ."

"Oh, please, Mr. Brown," pleaded Armour, "don't force it!" and there came a chorus from the class, "Don't force it, Mr. Brown," and subdued laughter, because we didn't know what forcing it was, anyway. "I assure you, gentlemen, I shall not force it until I have tried every expedient." A chorus of thanks and a renewed reverie. Then presently Mr. Brown would suddenly turn toward us and say excitedly:

"Did you try a function of m, Armour?"

"I never thought of it."

"It may resolve it." And away rattled Mr. Brown's chalk, line upon line, till there stretched the equation, solved! To us it looked bigger than ever.

I won't swear that it was a function of m that did the trick. It may have been one of the other mystic agents such as a "coefficient of x," or perhaps pi, a household word to us, as vague as it was familiar.

But what I mean is that when Mr. Brown said he could "force" an equation he referred to a definite mathematical process, as certain as extracting a square root and needing only time and patience.

What I am saying, then, is that school mathematics, and college mathematics as far as made compulsory, should be made up in great proportion, in overwhelming proportion, of straight calculation. I admit that the element of ingenuity, of individual discovery, must also count for something; but for most people even the plainest of plain calculations contain something of it. For many people the multiplication table is still full of happy surprises: and a person not mathematical but trained to calculate compound interest with a logarithm can get as much fun out of it as Galileo could with the moon.

Now to many people, mathematicians by nature, all that I have said about problems and puzzles is merely a revelation of ignorance. These things, they say, are the essence of mathematics. The rest of it is as wooden as a Chinese abacus. They would tell me that I am substituting a calculating machine for a calculating mind. I admit it, in a degree. But the reason for it is perhaps that that is all most of us are capable of. We have not been made "mathematically minded," and hence the failure of our mathematics.

I am of course stepping out here on ground where wiser feet might hesitate to tread. But I think that for most of us something goes wrong, very early in school, with our mathematical sense, our mathematical conceptions—or rather with the conceptions that we fail to get. We get lost in the symbols of mathematics and can't visualize the realities—visualize or dramatize, or whatever you do with them. Mathematics is always, for most of us, a sort of mystery which w don't even expect to understand. Let me illustrate the attitude by recalling a joke of a stage "review" of a few years ago. Some boys are seen coming out of school, comically overgrown and comically under-dressed, grown too long and dressed too short, so as to make them look funny.

"Well, my little man," says a stock stage gentleman, in the stock voice of a stage question, "and what are you learning at school?"

"Reading and writing," says one of the comedian boys, his immobile face a marvel of wooden imbecility, blank as the alphabet.

"Reading and writing," repeats the stock gentle-man, so as to let the audience get it, "and anything else?"

The "boy" answers, with no facial movement, "We learn gazinta."

"You learn what?"

"Gazinta."

"But what is gazinta?"

"Why," explains the boy, "like 'two gazinta four' and 'five gazinta ten.'"

The roar of the audience's laughter ends the mathe-matics. They laugh because in the contrast between the clarity of reading and writing and the mystery of "gazinta" they see their own experience. For them all mathematics is, and always will be, "gazinta."

Here is a particular example, familiar to all school and college people, of what I mean by our failure to get a proper grasp of mathematical thought. We all learn that the attraction of gravity exercised on or by a body varies in direct proportion to its mass, and inversely as the square of its distance. The square? That's the sticker for most of us. What's the square got to do with it? We understand, or we think we do, that of course the more "mass" a thing has the more it pulls. In reality this is the real philosophical difficulty, since mass means power to "pull," and "pull" means having mass. But we don't look into it so far as that; the bigger the mass, the bigger the pull, all right. But the square of the distance we accept, learn it by heart, use it, multiply it—in short, it becomes "gazinta." It seems an odd thing. Why the square? Why not the cube, or the anything else? We don't see, till we learn to get it straight, that the thing is self-evident.

The pull varies with the amount of *surface,* a thing of two dimensions, broad and long. A tower at a certain distance (don't call it *x* or we'll get mixed) looks a certain height and looks a certain breadth. A tower twice as far away would have to be twice as high to look level with it and twice as broad to look of the same breadth. So the far-away tower at twice the distance of the near one, in order to look the same size, would have to be twice as high and twice as broad and would present to the eye four square feet to one, in order to present an apparently equal surface. The attraction is in proportion to the surface and gets less and less for any given size of surface as you go further away. And it doesn't matter if the surface is square or round or triangular, or any other shape, since they are all proportional. Here I believe is where *pi* comes in—

but don't let us go too far with it.

There are ever so many of these mathematical conceptions that turned into mystification because we never got them right at the start. The trigonometrical ratios —sine, cosine, etc.—seemed just an arbitrary iniquity. If we had thought of them as moving arms, like traffic signs, we would have felt them to be the natural and inevitable way of measuring an angle.

. . . .

It seems to me therefore that something might be done, at the very opening of education, to strengthen our grip on the mathematical idea. This would bring us back, I presume, to those mathematical judgments synthetically *a priori* with which I started. The question involved is the nature of number and magnitude, and why does one and one make two? and the consideration whether a statement of that sort is just a fact or an inference from one judgment to another. I imagine that if we could see into one another's minds we should find a great difference in our grasp on the sequence of numbers. A hen, it is understood, can distinguish two from one but is lost at three. Primitive languages count a little way and then say "a whole lot." Here figures end and lies begin. Even the Greeks used to say "a myriad" to mean not an exact number but ever so many.

We have fallen heirs to the wonderful ingenuity of what we call Arabic notation. In reality the Hindus started it, but the Arabs made it plainer still by writing into it a "cipher" or "zero" to mark a blank place. We learn it so early in life and so artificially that we don't appreciate it. We think of ten as an arbitrary point, whereas the shift to a new "place" could have been set anywhere, and would be better if set at something more divisible than ten. If the people on Mars have brains as much better than ours as their planet is older, they may use a set of numbers that would go thousands at a jump and write the population of the United States in three figures. We couldn't of course do that. The multiplication table used for it would be beyond our learning. But I am sure that we, the nonmathematical people among whom I belong, would get a better grip on mathematics if we had a better conception of the relationship of numbers and symbols.

I am aware of course that there are many recent books that attempt to shed new light on mathematics. But the light seems dim. One or two well-known "series" contain what are really admirable presentations of the philosophy of mathematics. But, for the ordinary person, to mix philosophy with mathematics only makes it worse. Other popular works undertake to bring mathematics to the intelligence of the millions; it would be invidious to name the books, but, apart from their optimistic titles, I cannot see much success in them.

I am aware also that various new methods of teaching mathematics are adopted, especially in teaching mathematics to beginners. But in any that I have seen there is little else than one more example of the present tendency to turn children's education into fun. Kindergarten children waving little flags, forming themselves into squares and cubes and separating themselves into fractions, may look very pretty, but they are no nearer to the mysteries of number. Singing the multiplication table doesn't make it less relentless.

Here on my desk, for instance, is a widely known pretentious book of "new method." It undertakes to "individualize arithmetic" by teaching the children what the author calls "number facts" by the use of numbered cards. "Cards," says this authority, "are invaluable for learning number facts." Many of us found this out long ago. The children "individualize" their arithmetic by sitting in a ring, dealing out cards with numbers and pictures on them, and then seeing whose "number facts" win out against their opponents. The children might learn poker from this but not mathematics. What they are doing sounds like a "showdown" of "cold hands," a process as old as California.

The basic idea of my discussion is that somehow we don't get our minds mathematically adjusted as they might be. I am aware that there are great differences of natural aptitude. We are told that Isaac Newton when he was a boy took a look through Euclid's *Elements* and said it seemed a "trifling book." That meant that, when Euclid said, "the three angles of a triangle are together equal to two right angles," little Newton said, "Why, of course, obviously so." Probably the Pythagorean theorem about the squares on the sides of a right-angled triangle only held him back a minute or two. These things took the rest of us a year of school. But, all said and done, I think that it is not only a matter of aptitude but of approach. We don't "go at it" right.

With that I leave the subject, with the hopes that at least it may be stimulating to professors of mathematics. A little stimulant won't hurt them.

V

Parlez-Vous Français?

CHAPTER V

PARLEZ-VOUS FRANÇAIS?

or

WHY CAN'T WE LEARN MODERN LANGUAGES?

Sit down, Gentlemen — The annual mass attack on French and its repulse — How to learn French: forget English — Never learn a rule: learn to think subjunctively — Swallow the phrase whole — Read for reading's sake — When you get it, it's like swimming

I REMEMBER that when I was a student taking German at college, a criticism reached the ears of our good old professor to the effect that the students never spoke German and never heard it. He was hurt at this, and so at the end of that term he put on what was announced as an oral examination. We were directed, four at a time, into a little room, where the professor and two "outside examiners" were sitting in state as a board of examination.

I went in with three other students and we lined up across the room.

"Setzen Sie sich, meine Herren," said the professor, very impressively. This means, "Sit down, gentlemen."

We stood right there.

"Meine Herren," repeated the professor, as casually as he could, *"nehmen Sie, bitte, Platz."*

No, sir; not us; we never budged.

"Sit down, gentlemen," said the professor curtly.

Down we sat, all together.

After that year there weren't any more oral examinations.

.　　　.　　　.　　　.　　　.　　　.　　　.

The same thing could have happened in any North American university, and could have been carried out in any of the modern languages—except in French in French Canada. Yet any of us, with the instruction we received, could have translated ordinary German or French into English, and even put English sentences into French or German by a process like working with a hammer and saw.

I have selected French as the main object of discussion in this chapter because I have had over sixty years of dealing with it and enjoy the advantages for observation that go with residence in a bilingual province. But all that is said here about learning French could be said about learning German, Spanish, Russian or Norwegian.

The fault with our teaching of modern languages is not so much that we teach them wrongly as that we don't succeed in teaching them at all. Ask anyone who "took" Freshman French at college, or learnt French in high school. Only don't ask him in French.

Every year in English-speaking North America a vast phalanx of high school and college students, millions of them, gather for a mass attack on French. They come on against a heavy barrage of declensions, conjugations and exceptions; they are beaten back

gather again and re-form each year till their school-
days end in defeat—as glorious and as hopeless as
Pickett's charge at Gettysburgh. Twenty-five years
later, when the pupils and students have grown up into
adult life, there will be practically nothing left of their
French except a few fragments and a little wistful regret and wonder. Ask your friend, the father of a
family, what French he knows, and he will say that
he knows such things as, *"Donnez-moi un bock, s'il
vous plaît"* and *"Garçon, encore un bock."* But he
learned those on a trip to Paris, in the proper way,
by eating and drinking them in.

Let me speak here on my own experience, not from
vanity over it or egotism in telling it, but because I
think it is typical of that of thousands of others. I
learned, or mislearned, my French in the English-
speaking Province of Ontario; but what I say of Ontario, for which I have nothing but affection, is not directed against it singly. I am certain that its faults
are shared by practically all our English-speaking con-
inent. Of England I am not speaking for the moment;
over there the proximity of France and the fact that
languages were learned for generations before the
schools spoiled the process make things a little different. But not altogether so.

Let me then explain about my experience in Ontario. I am not offering here any criticism against the
efficiency and the industry of the many hundred people
who teach French in the schools of Ontario. They do
what they are compelled to do to meet the strange
and disastrous kind of test applied to their pupils.

They have to prepare their pupils to pass the matriculation examination of the universities; and they do so. Some of their pupils even pass with distinction; others carry away what is called honours, and are so badly damaged thereby for learning French that a residence of ten years in Paris would hardly effect a complete recovery of their native faculties.

And the amazing thing about the situation is that if Anatole France or Victor Hugo had been sent up to write on an Ontario matriculation examination in French there is not the slightest chance that either of them would head the list; they would be beaten right and left by girls from Seaford High School who never saw the red wings of the Moulin Rouge, and by boys from the Hamilton Collegiate Institute who wouldn't know enough real French to buy a boiled egg in the Café de la Paix. Indeed it is doubtful whether Anatole France and Victor Hugo would have passed at all. The whole examination being a test in English, they would probably have been ploughed and have had to be put under the care of an Ontario special teacher for six months to enable them to get through.

The point that I am endeavoring to make and reinforce with all the emphasis of which I am capable is this: the ability to translate French into English in writing is not a knowledge of French. More than this, it is the very opposite of it. It involves, if exercised persistently and industriously, a complete inability *ever* to have a knowledge of French. The English gets in the way. The French words are forever prevented from acquiring a real meaning in connection with the

objects and actions indicated, because the mind has
been trained always and for ever and hopelessly to associate them with English words instead of with things.
The process is fatal. The whole system is not only
worthless but it is a fraud and an imposition practised
upon all those who learn French in such a school
method; and the schools are driven to use the method
because the colleges impose a written examination of
translation and grammar as the criterion of a knowledge of French. For the proof of it I appeal to the
candid confession of all those who were trained in
this machine. I appeal to such people for corrobora-
tion of what I say. All that they learned was directed
toward nailing the English word so tight to the French
one that nothing can ever prize them apart.

I, myself, speak of what I know. When I was a little
boy in England I learned to use a few small phrases
in French, such as *"Bonjour, Monsieur"* and *"Au
revoir,"* in the proper and real way; not connecting
them with any link to English words but letting them
spring out of the occasion. Anybody who understands
the matter will understand what I mean. Later on I
learnt French in Ontario and entered, traversed, and
left the Provincial University with all sorts of distinction in it. Part of the teaching, like part of the curate's
egg at the Bishop's table, was excellent no doubt, but
the base of it was worthless; it had all been undermined and spoiled and forever rendered futile by the
unspeakable matriculation examination which preceded
it and which was a necessary preliminary to entrance to
the French classes.

I mean it literally and absolutely when I say that
I knew more French *in the real sense of knowing it*
when I was a child of six years in England than when
I was given first-class honours at graduation by the
University. In the first case I knew a little; in the
second case I knew not a single word that was not
damaged by false association and contact. All the
energy and industry and determination that I had put
into my college work, all the interest and fascination
that I felt for the language, all the pride that I could
have felt in really knowing and using it—was dashed
to pieces against the stone wall of the barrier erected
in my path.

When I graduated I could not use a single word of
French without thinking of English. I had to begin
painfully and wearily all over again at the very bottom. Somehow I had stumbled upon the secret of a
true beginning, and I began to try to collate in my
mind the French words and the objects and ideas and
to exclude the English. But it was hard work. The
college had left its fatal mark deep stamped upon my
brain. But at last, many years after my graduation,
and with advantage of residence in Montreal, the light
began to break.

If I live long enough to forget a little more of what
I learnt at school I shall soon be able to speak French
as well as a Montreal cab-man talks English. More
than that I do not ask. But for my academic education I might have spoken French with the easy fluency
with which the girls behind the notion counters of the
Montreal department stores rip off their alternative

languages. For such higher competence I can only have
a despairing admiration. It is not for me. Yet let me
speak as the cab-man and the car conductor speak, and
I am content to depart in peace. For I shall know that
if a French angel (such is the kind I should prefer)
opens the gate to me and says *"D'où venez-vous?"*
I shall answer *"Je viens de Montréal,"* without first
framing the thought in English.

Let us consider a little further the matter under
discussion. The whole of the teaching of school French
is directed toward passing the matriculation examination of the colleges. This examination is conducted on
paper in English. It has therefore absolutely no connection with the use of the ear as a means of hearing
language. In fact, the language is regarded as a thing
seen but not heard. I am told that people thus taught,
when they land at Calais or Dieppe, are often seen to
grasp their ears at the first tingling of the new sensa-
tion of hearing a language spoken. Moreover, the
examination in question consists, entirely, or almost so,
of writing out English translations of French words
and of translating written English words into French
ones.

The typical form of a French examination test is
to hand out to the candidate a rapid-fire series of silly-
looking little grammatical difficulties involving a queer
sequence of pronouns or something of the sort. Some
such exercise as this is given:

Translate into French:
Speak to us of it. Do not speak of it to them with

me. Let him have some of it for them. Lend it to us,
but do not lend it to them. Etc., etc., etc.

I should like to put Victor Hugo and a Montreal
cab-man down in front of this and see what utter hash
they would make of it. The truth is that ability to
do this kind of translation-gymnastics, this leaping in
and out in a kind of egg-shell dance among the pronouns, can only be accomplished at a dreadful expense
of damage in other directions. The wretched literalism
involved is absolutely fatal.

I do not say that a person who really knew French
and knew English could not translate these things. He
might. But the prospect would make him tired. And
probably in about half a page of this stuff he would
make a slip or two in whichever language was not his
mother tongue. But notice. The highly trained girl
from Seaforth High School who has never seen the
sails of the Moulin Rouge will make no slip at all.
She will translate with absolute accuracy every last one
of these rotten-looking sentences. Yet if the examiner
said to her in French, "My child, you have answered
admirably, come and have lunch with me at the Café
Américain," she would blush the ruby red of detected
ignorance.

But this juggling with pronouns and idioms is only
a part of the idiocy of the school translation system.
There is plenty more of it. The pupil is not only taught
to translate the ordinary common words that he would
really need if he were ever, poor soul, actually going
to use French, but he is taught right at the outset of

his instruction a string of words, or rather the translation of a string of words, that he is never conceivably going to use at all. Just because these words have a peculiar plural they are dragged in at the very opening of the pupil's acquaintance with the language. Most of them he will never see again, except of course on an Ontario examination paper.

Bal, carnaval, chacal, nopal, regal, cal, have, so it appears, irregular plurals. Who cares if they have? The way to learn an irregular plural is by happening to want to use the word often enough to learn it. That is the way in which an English child learns that the plural of *foot* is *feet,* and a French child that the plural of *bal* is *bals.* Similarly the words *bail, email, corail, soupirail, vantail, vitrail,* have irregular plurals. But what of that? Wait till one wants to use them or runs up against them in the course of speaking or reading French. It is awful, and it is futile, to learn them in a list; and it is still more awful to parade the list on an examination paper as if knowledge of it were a real test of the degree of attainment of a person learning French.

But since the examination has to be faced and since the examination is sure to contain some of these specimens as a test, the little books of instruction carry exercises that run:—

Have you the opals of the jackals?
No, but my father has the enamels of the leases.

This kind of thing used to give me the idea that French conversation must be awfully silly. The two

Frenchmen who had just asked about opals and jackals would suddenly break off in a terrible flurry to say:

"Where are the stained glass windows? Where are the folding doors?"

Many school-boys must have thought the French a peculiarly unstable people, incapable of fixed attention.

Or turn from nouns to verbs. The school pupil learns these in a list. The Montreal cab-man learns them by their use. When the school pupil proposes to say "We shall see" in French, he starts off from the English "to see"—French *voir;* future, *je verrai, tu verras, il verra*— Ha! ha!—he's getting near it now! *Nous verrons,* "we shall see"! Triumph! Now the cab-man (whether French by birth or English) has learned that group of sounds, *nous verrons,* in a lump, associated with the idea. Or else he hasn't learned it at all. But if he has, he knows it and uses it in the real true sense of language. The college matriculant, wanting to use it, stands dumb with a perfect fury of rapid conjugation boiling up in his mind till it boils over as *nous verrons*—half a minute too late for use.

. . . .

It might of course be claimed that even this defective method of teaching at least opens up the language as literature and leads the way to the study of its history and philology. People who never expect to talk French may still, it is claimed, enjoy the pleasure of reading the great masterpieces of French literature without a translation, and the advantage of reading the French books and journals of the hour for which there is no translation. There is of course something in this argument, but far less than one might suppose. Experience shows that people who have learned French without being able to pronounce it decently, without any power of understanding it by the ear and without the ability to read it without the English words showing through the French print, seldom go on reading it at all. For technical purposes they may puzzle it out; in rare cases—I have known such—they make of the unspoken, unheard language a sort of bridge to the literature of the past; but in the vast majority of cases such French, as far as culture goes, gets nowhere. The appreciation of literature is too dim, when the words are mere mechanical symbols lacking life; even parchments of philology rustle dry when a living language is thus numbered with the dead.

But let me turn from the negative to the positive. Finding fault is one thing, and improvement is another. So far, I admit, I have merely spoken of how *not* to learn a modern language. But I am prepared to go in the other direction and show how to learn it, with less difficulty, ever so much more reality and far happier results. I will undertake to teach anybody any modern language perfectly in five minutes—not the whole of it, which nobody ever knows, but just a little bit of it; and with that beginning he can go on as far as he likes. For example I would take him out from my house where I write this book and have him meet on the road an Ojibway Indian from the Reserve near by and call out to him *"Aneen! b'jou!"* After he had

said that quite a few times to quite a few Indians it
would begin to seem a natural thing to say to an Indian when you met him. After he had said it a year
or two he would go on saying it in his sleep. But if
he asked what do the words *mean*, I would not tell
him. If he starts breaking them into fractions of English, it's all over with Ojibway; all he needs to know
is that that is what you say when you say it.

The little bits of foreign language that we really
make our own—such as *carte blanche* and *pâté de foie
gras* and *eau de vie*—come to us just that way. English
is shut out; we never think of "white card" or of
"pastry of fat liver." Still less do we deliberately make
blanche feminine to fit with *carte*. In fact we don't
notice that it is feminine. A person fitting the genders
together gets left behind in conversation. Gender
forms are only things that you notice, and group together perhaps, after you begin to acquire the language. It is of no help whatsoever to learn them in
lists; each one must be *used* with any combination it
comes into. There is no royal road and no way of
shortening it.

I am not here merely advocating the use of what is
often called the "natural" method—the plan of learning languages by talking and hearing them. Few people
ever have the opportunity to talk them enough and
hear them enough to go very far. Few people can go
to France and stay there for ten years, and for people
at home "conversation" lessons, unsupported by any
other form of effort and instruction, break down of
their own weight. They begin in a burst of enthusiasm,

radually turn into something like annoyance. The
eacher is so fluent, the pupil so helpless, the sense of
rogress is soon changed for a sort of expanding hori-
on of ignorance. There comes a happy moment when
ie lessons are dropped, and nothing remains but *Bon
ur, Monsieur"* and *Oh, oui."*

Nor am I, for the present, trying to explain how
ie learning of French, or any other foreign language,
in be fitted in as a class exercise in school or col-
ge. What I am here talking of is how you get it into
our own head. In this, as in the whole scope of edu-
tion, it is overwhelmingly your own effort, your own
itiative that counts. What people learn best is what
ey teach themselves, what they learn of their own
rompting.

One recalls in the *Pickwick Papers* the statement
' Mr. Weller Senior that he had taken a good deal
pains with the education of his son by letting him
n in the streets when he was very young and shift for
mself. It is the grain of truth in this that makes it
nny, the incongruity between what appears to be ut-
r neglect but is described as calculated foresight. As
ual the humour turns on the revelation of truth by
congruous contrast. If the little Weller had had no
tive gift for seeing and learning, for storing up ex-
rience and profiting by it, the whole opportunity of
e streets would have been wasted on him. And if
tle Weller had attended a sociological class on Life
the Street (half course, half term, one credit), he
ould have been unfitted to live on them.

The beginning of learning is the urge to learn. The

teacher and the class exercise are just a supplement and a help, but never can be the motive power. Wisdom cannot be poured into the pupil out of a jug. What I have in mind is a process that supplements any conversation method used, and any reading done—a process, carried on in one's own mind, of excluding one's own native language, of setting up a direct connection between the sound of the words and the things and actions that they stand for. A person trained in this way, if he cannot express himself in the foreign language, can at least be *silent* in it; what is meant is that his own language, English let us say, will not rise up in his mind and choke him. That is why cab-men, hotel waiters and ticket collectors seem to talk French so easily. Nothing else comes into their minds. If they're stuck for a word or a phrase they must find one; but at least no English will "butt in" as it would with us.

But before developing this idea more fully I want first to indicate how very great, in the learning of languages, are the limitations of what can be accomplished by ordinary people in ordinary circumstances. A great deal of misunderstanding and myth and legend surround the acquisition of foreign languages. People of humble minds outside of academic circles imagine that there are various other people who speak half a dozen languages perfectly. As a matter of fact there are none, and never have been except on the plan explained above for the use of the Ojibway language—perfect as far as it goes.

We read in history of the famous Scottish scholar,

the "Admirable" Crichton of three centuries ago, that he possessed twelve languages and that once when journeying to Paris he invited "the university" to meet him in disputation at nine o'clock on such and such a morning when he would be ready to dispute in any one of them. We are told by Milton that a man may pick up the Italian tongue in an odd hour. Similar myths run all down our history and are matched by current references to people who can speak three or four languages perfectly, and especially to Russians to whom an extra language is an easier matter than an extra suit of clothes. I remember having been told of an official interpreter in a magistrate's court in Toronto who had to deal with nondescript Europeans of all sorts of languages. He had such a gift for languages that if a man turned up whose language he didn't know he would ask the magistrate for a couple of days' delay and then go home and learn the language. It sounds easy, doesn't it?

Unfortunately the learning of a language is a much more arduous matter than that. It must begin in a humble way with nouns and phrases—never with grammar and sentences. And from the very beginning the learner, and here everything depends on himself and not on the teacher, should try to connect the foreign word (sound and letters) with the thing, the idea, that it stands for and to break it away from what appears to be its English equivalent. As a matter of fact there are probably no two words that are exact equivalents in two different languages. A *house* is not *une maison* and a *hotel* is not always *un hôtel*. Drinks

in America are sometimes said to be "on the house
they are never *"sur la maison."* A French duke,
matter how impoverished, always tries to keep a ho
in the city. An English duke, no matter how ri
refuses to.

Words and phrases are the beginning. But they m
be carefully divorced from grammar and grammati
rules about changes for the plural and so on. The
things come later on, as they did in learning our o
language in infancy. Most of us can remember rea
ing out of a grammar that "oxen, children and brethr
make the plural in n," and thinking: "Why, so th
do! How interesting!" Tables of verbs will nev
teach a person to say *je viendrai,* and *je verrai,* and
voudrais; you have to know them first, word by wo
bit by bit, and afterwards looking over a table of the
helps to give them a sort of consistency.

The case is still stronger with phrases. To anal
them out and put English to them spoils them
French. In nearly all phrases there is not one sin
English equivalent for the French or one single Fren
equivalent for the English. Take the most overwork
phrase in the French language, that joy of the c
versational tourist, *"Ça ne fait rien."* This mea
word by word, "That doesn't make nothing," and
sense, "That doesn't matter; that makes no differen
it's all the same to me; not at all, my dear chap; tha
all right"—and so on for a page. A person who l
learned to say *"Ça ne fait rien,"* as arising from
cumstances and not from translation, is already talki
French.

The most extreme case of the futility of translation
thods is found in the use of moods and tenses, as in
: employment of the subjunctive. This, for us, is the
›st difficult thing in the grammar of a foreign lan-
ıge because in English we have almost lost the sub-
ıctive—that is, almost forgotten how to *think* in
: subjunctive. Patriots are often trained to "think
ɔerially." Linguists have to be trained to "think sub-
ıctively." In English we have drifted so far away
›m the use of the subjunctive that our sense of its
ue has grown dim. It is like a lost or decaying fac-
y, as is the sense of smell in the human race. In
glish we put everything into the indicative mood as
t was a *fact*. We write, "They say that he is very
ı"—whether we mean that he really is, or only that
ɔple claim he is. We say, "They charged against
:rates that he was corrupting the youth of Athens."
Greek or a Roman would interject, "Do you mean
t that is what they charged, or that that is what he
s really doing?"
ı French the indicative has to some extent replaced
subjunctive but scarcely at all as compared with
glish. French people can still *feel* a subjunctive.
ıen they say, *"Il faut qu'il soit bien méchant,"* they
not saying that he *is* a bad lot, but only that he
ıld have to be to fulfill certain conditions. English
ple in talking French try to work out subjunctives
m a rule, without ever having really got the idea
:hem. I remember hearing an English lady at Calais
uest a custom's official to let her pass with the
rds, *Permettez, monsieur, que je passasse."* The

polite Frenchman bowed and said, *"Passassiez, Ma-dame."* The lady moved on with a gratified feeling of bilingualism achieved. A friend of mine once told me that in leading up to a proposal to a very charming French girl, he asked her if she would mind crossing the ocean. She replied, *"Ah, non! si j'étais avec quelqu'un qui me fît oublier les ennuis du voyage."* His astonishment and admiration of her use of the preterite subjunctive struck him silent so long that he lost her. Two lives went astray over a lost mood.

English people can, with effort and difficulty, reac-quire the subjunctive sense. But if not, the only thing to do is to go ahead without it; trample it down and forget it. After all no Frenchman, and few Irishmen, can ever learn to use *shall* and *will*. The subjunctive must either be used instinctively and through the sense of it or left alone. Seen in this light how terrible is such a thing as a "grammatical exercise" beginning with the dictum, "In French, verbs of *fearing, avoid-ing, denying, forbidding,* etc., etc. govern the subjunc-tive. *Ne* is inserted before the verb in the subordinate clause to indicate an affirmative conclusion; *ne pas,* to indicate a negative." Then follows an exercise. Trans-late: "I am afraid he is coming. I am not afraid he is coming. I am afraid he is not coming. I am not afraid he is not coming." Enough of that stuff puts a student of languages beyond resuscitation.

The time comes presently when the pupil in learn-ing French on a proper method may begin to read it. And here again the secret of learning is to try to say good-bye to the English translation as rapidly a possible. *"Le Petit Chaperon Rouge"* is what the French call our "Little Red Riding Hood." But having said "Little Red Riding Hood" once in this connection, never say it again. Call up the vision of the little girl picking flowers in the wood, her red cloak falling back from her shoulders, and connect with the picture the words *Le Petit Chaperon Rouge*. Learn what a little bit of the French story means and say it over and over again; get it away from the English and as you go further on with reading never bother as to what a French word "means" (in English) provided you can hit the general sense and go on. Better one half the sense in French than all of it in English.

When you read French in this way there will come a time when you find that you can read it, more or less straight ahead, without thinking of English. It is like learning to swim. It comes to you, after the hard initial effort that made it possible, with a warm glow of accomplishment. After that the language is yours. You have set up in your mind a division into compartments in one of which is English, in the other French. Henceforth they will not interfere. When you read French in this way a lot of the words will carry vague meanings that gradually clarify; but it doesn't matter much whether they do—just as, in English, people go on reading sea stories all their lives without knowing what the "lee-scuppers" are except that people fall into them, or whether the "binnacle" is what the captain sits in or where the men sleep.

The French speech of a person trained in this proper way and the French writing of a person properly

taught are necessarily for a long time filled with i
accuracies; children in learning to talk English at fir
are apt to run their words to a pattern, for examp
to make all the verbs "weak"—to say, "I bited tl
apple," "He sawed me coming," and so on. This clea
away of itself, not by learning rules but by continuo
and unconscious imitations.

But what is utterly unnatural is the false and ove
done standard of excellence of the student of Fren
in a grammar class, writing out twenty sentences
subjunctives without an error, finding feminines f
blanc, for *beau,* for *turc,* for *tourangeau* and so fort
as easily as picking flowers. The method of teachi
French here shares in the fault that goes with all e
amination discipline—the pressure to put on the la
increment of excellence that only comes at an inor
nate cost, an inordinate sacrifice of other things.
steamer whose economic speed is sixteen knots can p
haps be forced up to twenty at a double cost, and ev
beyond that, at an expense utterly disproportionate.
pupil who takes over ninety per cent in French gra
mar is like a little tug raising enough steam to mo
a freighter, at the expense of being all boiler and
cargo.

I admit the full difficulty of turning what is he
said to its practical application in re-forming the cu
riculum of a school. But just as the fear of the Lo
is the beginning of wisdom, so a clear sense of wh
is desired, of the goal to be achieved, will sooner
later find the means of achievement. But even witho
attempting in any degree to lay down a school curric

lum in French, one or two generalities may at least be
hazarded. Students ought to begin with nouns and
names, learned off picture-placards by the oral method
of fifty years ago—spelling and sound together. Follow these pictures by phrases, and plenty of them,
learned as far as possible without connection with
English: *Voici un hibou; Voilà un cheval.* . . . Steal
from bygone Ollendorf one or two question-and-answer forms endlessly repeated: *Voyez-vous le cheval!
Oui, je vois le cheval.* . . . Let at least all class-room
directions be in French: *Asseyez-vous.* . . . *Fermez
la porte.* . . . *Écoutez bien.* . . . And exhort the
student at the start to try to get away from his own
language.

A little further on comes reading out loud by the
teacher; here enters such a story as *Le Petit Chaperon
Rouge*—the English of it only explained once, just as
little as is necessary, and then endless repetition of the
reading. Dictation of French, to be written and spelled
by the students as best they can and turned back and
forward into Ollendorf questions, is a true linguistic
discipline, the best there is, and the one, I imagine,
the most nearly abandoned by our colleges in their entrance tests. And most of all it is necessary to realize
that a percentage examination, carried on in writing,
and calling for a false degree of excellence in detail,
in this as in nearly every other part of education, spells
frustration and defeat. But of that I speak in more general and fuller terms in another chapter.

In what I have said about the teaching of French
I have been referring to the situation in North Amer-

ica—the United States and Canada—where it is probably the worst in the world. The whole power of a
vast, expensive and enthusiastic public education is here
directed along false lines of effort. In Liberia, where
they make no effort at all, I am sure they do it better.

In England for various reasons the situation is different from ours. The proximity of France across the
Channel, the fact that thousands of people learn their
French from actual contacts and the fact that "native" teachers are everywhere available counts for
much. So too does the fact that French was widely
taught in England before the era of modern "translation" text-books, before analytical sentence-translation
and was taught largely in phrases and on a "natural"
method. Even the earlier translation texts were not
like ours. If anyone will glance at the famous Ollendorf of a hundred years ago he will see that it aims
at a constant repetition of similar French forms by
means of questions and answers. *"Avez-vous le chapeau
de mon père?" Non, Monsieur, je n'ai pas le chapeau
de votre père."*

Ollendorf seems to be wrong in admitting English
as the medium. But the intention of his famous
"method" was that the pupil would, by the repetition
system, jump out of English to French; each French
sentence would suggest a new one; each French thought
would reproduce itself in a slight variation. *"Avez-
vous mangé votre déjeuner?" "Non, Monsieur, je n'a
pas encore mangé mon déjeuner."*

It has been only more recently that up-to-date text

books on the model of their own begin to swamp out older and better methods.

Now the English are naturally the worst linguists in the world, but they carry down from their insular history the remains of a contempt for foreign nations, including foreign languages. The Eskimos are accustomed to call themselves "the people" and the English in many things share the Eskimo attitude. This sense of superiority, in point of language, carries advantages and disadvantages. English people are apt to consider that they "know French" when they are able to pass a few phrases back and forward across the lunch counter at Dieppe, or call out in a confident voice, *"Garçon, l'addition, s'il vous plaît!"* They are seldom interested in shades of pronunciation; they pronounce *tenez* and *savez* as if written in English *tenny* and *savvie* (to rhyme with "many" and "navvy"), and are willing to let it go at that. On the other hand, use and custom have enabled them to grasp far more easily than we do what a Frenchman is trying to say and to answer him with some such apposite phrase as *"Très bien, Monsieur"* or *"Cela ne fait rien."*

I remember, as an illustration of this attitude, the visit to my university, McGill, about forty years ago, of André Siegfried, then an unknown and inquiring young Frenchman, since known to all the world. He stood and talked in easy effortless French to one of my elderly colleagues, an Englishman of the Oxford type. As Siegfried talked my colleague stood first on one foot and said, *"Oui—oui—oui—ah, oui,"* and then on the other foot and said, *"Oh, non—non—non,"* and then back to *oui*. Afterwards I heard him telling of the interview: "Delightful young man, speaks really excellent French. We chatted away for a long time—all in French, of course."

This easy unconsciousness of the very problem of language gives a sort of reality to French in England, vastly different from the anxious, pathetic failure of French in America.

As a matter of fact, a full mastery of even two languages is a very rare thing. It can only come as the result of a special environment, the opportunity to talk both, the will to do so, and therewith a certain aptitude. What is ordinarily thought as bilingualism falls away below this.

Compare, for example, the "bilingual" city of Montreal, of whose one million people, some seven out of ten are French. All the French people of any education understand English, and all of them speak it in a way to make themselves easily understood for business and for ordinary conversation. But with a very few exceptions their speech falls far short of the range and power of people speaking their own language. They can say what they mean but they can neither adorn nor embellish it. Their pronunciation, of course, while pleasing enough, is not the same as ours; it may be better but it is not the same. Even their understanding of English of necessity falls short in point of appreciation of our literature; so much depends, especially in poetry and in the drama, on the full connotation of the words, the shades of meaning which they have taken on with us from infancy.

Can a foreigner fully distinguish the curfew "tolls the knell of parting day" from "rings the six o'clock bell"? Can he feel the appeal of a tide that "drew from out the boundless deep" and "turns again home"? "In Flanders fields the poppies blow!" Can any foreigner appreciate the delicacy of *blow?* We have no measure of the intimacy of their comprehension, but it is not unfair to doubt it.

As to the bilingualism of the English people of Montreal there is hardly any of it. Most of them learn a little French in school, recognize a lot of French words, especially those on sign-boards and know that "Guy Street!" as called out by the bilingual car-conductor is in French "Ghee!" The exceptions are too few to matter. Yet here is a city where an unobservant visitor, haunted by a myth, would say, "In Montreal, of course, everybody talks both English and French."

People who have devoted attention to the subject of foreign languages may be inclined to differ from me as to their valuation of translation. They may argue that translation represents as it were the last word, the supreme exercise in language. The extraordinary difficulty of finding idiom for idiom, of carrying over from one language to the other an absolute identity of meaning with an equal excellence of diction, such difficulty is only matched by the attraction of doing it.

Now this is quite true. But such translation comes at the end not at the beginning of study.

VI

Has Economics Gone to Seed?

CHAPTER VI

HAS ECONOMICS GONE TO SEED?

*Economists end to end — Knowledge that falls asleep
— Political Economy as world gospel — The bottom
falls out of it — The Spendthrift saves society — Bad
money saves national trade — The colleges meet the
situation — A catalogue of dead opinion — Economists
dig in behind a barrage of x and y — Economics joins
the Chinese Classics*

SOME years ago when I was the dinner guest of a famous club in Boston, the chairman of the evening introduced me in the following words: "Our guest tonight is an economist. I need hardly remind you, gentlemen, of the large part played in our life of today
by our economists. Indeed it has been calculated that
if all the economists were laid out in a line, end to
end, starting at the Mexican border, they would
reach"—the orator paused impressively and added—
"nowhere."

That, I say, was a few years ago. What was a genial
joke then is plain fact now. In my opinion that is exactly where college economics stands. At a time when
the world is in danger of collapse from the dilemma
of wealth and want, the college economists can shed
no light—or rather only a multitude of cross lights that
will not focus to a single beam—in place of a light-

house, wreckers' signals, or, at best, fireworks, elaborate and meaningless.

The time has come to ask, has economics run to seed? Consider what we mean by the phrase. There comes a time in the life of plants and flowers, when bloom and freshness have passed away. The blossoms are gone, the green of bud and leaf has withered to a faded brown; on the shrivelled stem once bright with bloom there remains nothing but the ragged seed-pods, sear and unsightly. In these, indeed, lies resurrection, the hope of future life, but, for the moment, use, purpose and beauty are gone. Let the wind scatter the seed for a new start on other ground.

So it is with the growth of human knowledge. It rises in new force, vigorous in life, brilliant in expression and beneficent in power. Time passes. New growth has stopped. Knowledge, like a withering stick, becomes rigid and formal. Adaptability has gone. Leaf has become wood; speculation has turned to authority. The doddering thought has run to seed. The hand that holds the pen is dead.

So it was vast centuries ago when the Chinese, a brilliant nation in the sunrise of intellectual growth, invented a system of symbols, of little pictures, that permitted the written communication of thought. It was a marvellous advance. But over these little pictures the Chinese fell asleep for five thousand years, mumbling and reciting the "sacred books," sacred only in their primitive simplicity, like an idiot among savages.

The Babylonians measured out the sky and baked

their knowledge on clay, in wedge-shaped characters. They moved, stopped—and then the Assyrian came down like a wolf on the fold and Babylon was buried in the sand.

In Alexandria the new Greek science and medicine ran its course for over five hundred years. There the Ptolemies built a great library of half a million books, a lighthouse four hundred feet high with beams focused far out at sea, a wonder of the world. Here were the triumphs of Euclid, of Aristarchus and of Galen. Then knowledge slowly crystallized; life and inquiry died out of it; the great weight of opinion of the dead suffocated the living. The conquering Arab overran it all, and the Caliph Omar burned its books in the name of a Mohammedan God.

When Greece and Rome declined, the Barbarians came, but among them grew up the schools of the Christian church, the schools of Alfred and Charlemagne, like beautiful little plants in the forest. These grew into the cloistered learning of the monastery, copying its parchment books in the quiet of a scriptorium, a sanctuary all still within, noise and battle without. Then the learning of the church, over-weighted and encrusted with age, turned to scholasticism, substituting words for things and grammar for thought, formal and worthless.

The Renaissance swept all this away, to put in its place the "humanities" and the classical scholarship which was the mainstay of our learning and our literature in England and America for three hundred years. The education of a "gentleman" was based on conjugations and declensions; young ladies' minds were sweetened and enriched with Greek mythology, and America named its rising towns from the Rome and Syracuse of antiquity.

As the modern world of industry and machinery and democracy grew up, the world of classical education failed to notice that it was there and dozed quietly to rest, murmuring Latin quotations in its sleep.

As it slept, there rose up beside it, alert and eager with life, the new science of political economy. This, as fashioned by Adam Smith and Ricardo and their American disciples, seemed a wonderful dogma, fit to rank with Galileo's telescope and Isaac Newton's apple. It was so simple that it could all be written in a few pages. It told the poor exactly why they were so. Work, industry, liberty, free competition and a police force were all that was needed for social welfare. Every man got what he was worth and was worth what he got, and the world went of itself.

Not that this bright new dogma was taught in the colleges. Gentlemen didn't need it and the poor couldn't afford it. But the Cobdens and the Brights and the Manchester School put it round the world. It seemed like a gospel of light. Russian nihilists in the Siberian mines hid copies of John Stuart Mill under their shirts, like early Christians with a gospel.

Of teaching, I say, there was little. The East India Company first taught political economy in their college at Haileybury. Their cadets were supposed to need it, to work it on the Hindu. The first lecturer was Malthus, the apostle of the empty cradle; but he had

a hare-lip; the students couldn't understand him; so
no harm was done. In Scotland also political economy
was taught in college before and after Adam Smith;
not under that name but as a branch of philosophy and
the theory of moral sentiments. As such it turned into
a sort of dream, like philosophy itself, bankrupt since
Plato but garrulous as an aged patient in a workhouse
ward. When political economy joined it, that made
two. But as far as political economy meant practical
precept—work, save and take what you can get—the
Scotch didn't need it in school. They had it as home
work.

With the modernization of our education which began about fifty years ago, economics came sweeping in
as a college-subject. Students cried for it. Benefactors
died for it. It reached and swelled till it filled a B.A.
curriculum, turned into a graduate study and after that
students could go to Germany and get more of it, and
keep on with it until they died.

But even then, though no one realized it, the bottom
was out of it. Political economy had taken too much
for granted. Property, and above all property in land.
Where did that come from? asked Henry George. And
inheritance? Loosen the dead hand and let us see what
it holds in its fingers. What? Is that fair? All that
vast wealth! And labor, asked Karl Marx, does it get
all it produces? If so, why hire it? And competition,
asked a thousand complaining voices, as the complexity
of our machine industry grew, why is competition fair,
if the strong can crush the weak and vested interest
take its toll of necessity?

Even the theory of the matter turned upside down
like a capsized boat. Does cost of production really
govern the value of a thing, or does the value of a
thing dictate its cost? And with that the theorists
were off to a new start, perplexed as Milton's arguing
devils, who "found no end in wandering mazes lost."
Thus did the experts wrangle and jangle in their own
Paradise Lost. With the new century, economics, with
the bottom knocked out of it, was carried forward
floating on the mud, like Stephenson's first railway.

As a result, economic science has got itself into the
tangle in which it is tied today. Of all the "economic
truths" of a hundred years ago, I do not know of one
—literally, not of one—that would pass unchallenged.
Lord Bacon tells us that Pontius Pilate asked in jest
"What is truth?" and "would not stay for an answer."
If he asked the question of the economists of today
and waited for an answer, he would have to arrange
his board for a long time in advance.

Nothing stands. John Stuart Mill was convinced
that "productive labor" was the basis of social welfare—that and nothing else. Labor spent on producing
mere luxuries was wasted. The spendthrift was an
enemy to society. What he did was to call for velvet
clothes and champagne. Mill was a simple man, and
a velvet suit and a bottle of champagne seemed to him
the last word for a wild time. We could show him
something now. But the idea was that Mill's spendthrift, by calling for workmen to make him his suit
and fix his drink, diverted them from producing real
things that do not pass away—such as bridges, ma

chines and factories. "A demand for commodities," said Mill, "is not a demand for labor." This he made one of his "four fundamental propositions" that held up the whole structure like the pillars of the mediaeval firmament.

But where is the argument today? Smashed to fragments. The loudest of our complaints are the voices calling for more spending of money. Anything to start it going. Prime the pump. Pension the old men. Give everybody in Alberta $25 a month. Don't produce, spend. Cut production down, limit it. Let the hog die unborn and pay the farmer for the corn he doesn't raise, on the sole condition that he will spend the money and not save it.

There again, saving! That, with all the economists from Adam Smith to his latest imitator, was the prime force in progress. There the interest of the individual and of society focused to a single light. If everybody worked hard and saved money, then everybody would get rich, the future would be provided for, and rainy days be stalled off till every place would be as good as Nevada.

They never stopped to ask what happens if everyone sells and nobody buys—if we save enough to build so many machines that there's nothing for them to do. What if we do provide for the future? It hasn't come yet. How are we to get along till it does? Hence all the wrangle and jangle over "technology," technological improvement and technological unemployment, the waste of abundance and the superfluity of productive power.

I am not proposing to unravel the tangle—only to indicate it, coiled all over the ground on which we try to advance. In fact, it begins to look as if a "rainy day" were one of the best things in nature, and the more sudden the shower the better. Come on, loosen up and spend something! Have a cigarette.

So it seems that the bottom is out of the saving theory. That particular pillar is undermined and falling over. You may for the moment help yourself by saving money, but you're a poor pup in the social sense if you do. Go and buy a velvet suit and order a quart of extra dry.

Saving money! And there again the moment you say "money," off goes another explosion and up into the air a whole new mass of charred fragments. Scarcely a sentence is left intact of the old monetary theory that seemed as solid as bedrock. There it lay, the basis of our economic life and international trade —the doctrine of sound money. It seemed as if half the economic evils of the past had come about for lack of the knowledge and practice of it. Every student read in his economic scriptures of the evil of the Continental Dollar, the madness of the French Assignat and of how the Greenback was fought, slain and redeemed, as the dragon was fought by St. George.

Where is all this theory now? Nothing left, after the war explosion that blew it up, nothing except fierce hot blasts of contrary opinion rushing into the vacuum. Monetary theory, or at least monetary practice, denounces solid, sound money, and calls for money at least as bad as and if possible worse than that o other nations. "If you devalue your pound, remember we'll devalue our dollar. You can't work that stuff on us!" To cling to sound money would be to become a Christian all alone in the arena.

Of all these doctrines I am not attacking one. Of all these problems I am not solving any. I am only drawing attention to the hopeless muddle in which economic thought and practice has involved itself. It has become a mass of contradiction. Every nation is calling in one breath for freer trade and economic nationalism, for a sound currency as debased as possible, for rigid economy with plenty of spending—in other words, calling out, "High!" "Low!" "Up!" "Down!" "Begin!" "Stop!"—till all is a mere babel of voices.

Perhaps the best index of what has happened to the science of economics is what has happened to the teaching of it in our colleges. The colleges have a system for meeting such difficulties.

When opinion gets confused—living opinion—the colleges can always fall back on the opinion of the dead. If living men can't think, let's have a catalogue of all that dead men ever thought, and the students can learn that. In fact, economics can be all dosed up with history, as doctors dose a patient with iron. And statistics. If we don't understand the industrial world, at least let us have statistics. The continental area of the United States is 3,026,789 square miles and the number of spindles in Lowell, Mass., is 201,608 (or is it?) That's the stuff. Make a four-year course and give a degree in it—a D.F.

And with that, of course, goes the familiar therapeutics of putting in "qualifications," what is called the "relative" view—that a thing is partly so and partly isn't so. Any book of what is called "general economics," after indicating the continental area of the United States and the number of spindles in Lowell, Mass., proceeds to a series of propositions as to why wages partly rise and partly don't, why prices may fall, or perhaps leap up, proving that black is in a sense white, except that where it is white it is partly black. This course is called Economics 1. From it you get to first base.

And, most of all, if we can't understand it, let's at least see that outsiders don't. Let us dress economics up in esoteric language, give it a jargon of its own and break away from plain terms like labour and profit and money and poverty. Let's talk of "categories" and "increments" and "margins" and "series." Let's call our appetite for breakfast our consumer's marginal demand. That will fool them. And if I buy one cigar but won't buy two, call that my submarginal saturation point for nicotine.

Above all, let us call in the help of the psychologist. He's the fellow with the technique. Turn him onto the theory of value, and grandfather Adam Smith won't know his own offspring.

Accordingly, the theorist of today, following in the tracks of the dead scholasticism, the lost Babylonia and the Egyptian dozing in the dust of the pyramids, runs his economics to finer and finer distinctions that have lost all meaning for everyday life. He can no longer talk of our wants; he must have marginal wants, degrees of wants, increments of satisfaction, curves of desire meeting in an equilibrium. The difference as between plain language and this jargon is as between digestion and a stomach-ache. To the college economist a boy standing in front of a pastry shop represents a submarginal increment of satisfaction. Give him ten cents and he comes out with a consumer's surplus in him. You can see it sticking out.

If anyone thinks this argument overdone, this language strained, let him open with me the latest of the books on pure economic theory, the books that have such titles as the *Theory of Value, of Capital, of Investment,* anything like that. It would be invidious to name them singly since this is an attack not on a man but on a method.

Here before me on my desk is one of the latest, a book that will be pronounced by the reviewers as one of the really "big" things—an "outstanding contribution," that's the phrase. The ordinary person can no more read it than he can read Chinese. Here is a sample of how this outstanding contribution stands out:

The slope of the curve passing through any point p *has indeed a very definite and important meaning. It is the amount of* y *which is needed by the individual in order to compensate him for the loss of a small unit of* x. *Now the gain in utility got by gaining such an amount of* y *equals amount of* y *gained multiplied by marginal utility of* y; *the loss in utility got from losing the corresponding amount of* x *equals amount of* x *lost multiplied by marginal utility of* x (*so long as the*

quantities are small). Therefore, since the gain equal.
the loss, the slope of the curve

$$= \frac{am't \ of \ \text{y} \ gained}{am't \ of \ \text{x} \ lost} = \frac{marg'l \ utility \ of \ \text{x}}{marg'l \ utility \ of \ \text{y}}$$

The author naïvely adds:

"Have we any further information about the shape
of the curves?"

No, I hope not.

I was once the guest of that merry institution, the
Savage Club of London. Among the mock stunts o
the evening was a speech supposedly in Chinese with
an interpreter to explain it. After the bogus Chinese
guest had spoken about half a dozen sentences, the
chairman politely interrupted, and asked of the inter
preter, "Now, what has Mr. Woo-hoo said?" "Noth
ing, so far," said the interpreter.

The same is true of the quotation. It only mean
that when you have enough, you don't want any more

A thousand chapters have been written similar to
that sample. Take enough of that mystification and
muddle, combine it with the continental area of the
United States, buttress it up on the side with the his
tory of dead opinion and dress it, as the chefs say
with sliced history and green geography, and out of i
you can make a doctor's degree in economics. I have
one myself.

VII

Psychology the Black Art of the College

CHAPTER VII

PSYCHOLOGY THE BLACK ART OF THE COLLEGE

The Black Art in all ages — Hypnotism enters college — Psychology's department store — Deep Thought counter — Minds tested free — Psychology and school education — Child expression by ink-throwing — The Psychology of Salesmanship looks the Prospect in the eye — Intellectual test for Willie Worm as a calliper

AMONG the arts in every age there is one that is the Black Art—mysterious, fearsome, a thing to dread. The Black Art comes and goes—now this, now that. Savages have their Black Arts of incantations, Voodoo rites and medicine men. Earlier Christianity had its attendant devils, its witches and its sorcerers. Along the edges of the light that it gave the world was a dark cloud of superstition, fear, exorcism, persecution, terror. The early learning had its astrologer, in a cone-shaped cap and a gown figured with the Zodiac, pointing with his finger at horoscopes and disasters. But time turned him into a professor of astronomical physics, quite harmless. Beside him was the alchemist, working with crucibles, to transform lead to gold, and seeking the Elixir of Life. He was an awesome being, but has faded long since into a high school chemistry teacher, not so much concerned with how to live forever, as with how to live next winter. As Christianity dropped its devils and its daily miracles and its exorcisms, it faded, for college purposes, into "comparative religion," a first-year subject, popular as a snap. Students elect religion as cheerfully as they did in Scotland three hundred years ago. And it never fails them.

But a Black Art there has to be. Somewhere plain truth must fade to mystery; somewhere life must meet its border line; somewhere mind and matter present their irreconcilable contrast. Where one art abandons this shuddering mystery, another takes it up. One can see the Black Arts of the past and present moving and changing like the belts of light and shadow in an electric sign. Some day physics, that began in the sunlight of the new solar system as the very embodiment of clarity and fact and measured space and ponderated matter, may be the Black Art. For with the breaking of the atom, the disappearance of solidity, the change of matter into force, the old mystery is all back again and ready for a new astrologer.

But at the present hour and in the colleges all around us psychology has turned into the Black Art.

Now when I was at college, fifty years ago, psychology was an entirely innocuous subject. It was taught by a venerable professor in a long black gown—all senior professors at that date had to be venerable— and he taught it as he had imported it in the wood straight from Scotland thirty years or so before. I didn't take the subject myself but those of us outside of it understood that it dealt with such things as the "association of ideas" and whether mind was just a form of matter or matter merely a form of mind and how the mind "worked." It seemed quite harmless. It ranked along with ethnology, and the brand-new subject, just imported to Canada, political economy, as things by which students could take honours without having had a long previous training, like the five days a week in Greek for four years that made us "honour matriculants" in classics, able to translate four or five lines of Homer without stopping. It never seemed then that the lean kine of psychology and economics would one day eat up the fat, and pick the dead bones of Greek.

But there existed then, outside of college, in the dark, a mysterious and evil thing called "hypnotism." This wasn't *taught*. It was practised by "professors," far from venerable, and exhibited at ten cents a seat in third-rate public halls. The "professor" invited members of the audience to step up on the platform and be "hypnotized" and put through various antics. The audience didn't know whether it was jest or earnest, all faked up, or all real, or partly both. Certainly the exhibitions always contrived to have a certain amount of buffoonery like the "comic relief" of our ten-twenty-thirty theatre.

I went one night with four or five fellow students to such an exhibition. The "professor" appeared on a stage, with a row of empty chairs, and a background of ropes and pulleys and apparatus grimly mediaeval. He invited members of the audience to step up. I asked my fellow students if they would step up with me. All but one refused. They had a wholesome contempt for hypnotism and a secret fear of it. Curley Wood, who went on the platform with me, was a nervous-looking youth who lived on cigarettes.

We were given two end seats, and various other "subjects" came clumping up onto the platform. The "professor" then announced that he would look into the eyes of each subject and decide whether he was hypnotizable. He began with me as end-man. He stooped forward and looked fixedly in my eyes. I didn't like it. I was sorry I had come up. I wanted to get out of it. Then I remembered that in the Middle Ages the devil couldn't reach you if you kept reciting the *pater noster* in Latin. I didn't know that but I started reciting to myself the 47th proposition of Euclid, about the square on the hypotenuse. That beat the "professor." "You can step down," he said. I did, with a great gladness.

He looked at Curley's eyes and Curley turned as pale as his own cigarettes. "You can stay," said the "professor." He kept a few others. To judge by the absurd things he presently made them do—too absurd for likelihood—I should imagine they were hand-picked. But Curley Wood wasn't; there was no collusion in his case. Yet the "professor" seemed able to take a mortgage on his will power. "Tell the audience your name," he said. "Curley Wood," answered my fellow student quite clearly. "Now try to tell it to them again and *you can't*," said the "professor" with a Rosicrucian gesture. Curley couldn't. *Vox faucibus haesit.*

"Now I'll throw a rope round you and drag you to

this side of the stage. Resist if you like, but you'll have to come." . . . All that and more, till at last he let Curley go and a tom-fool comic effect replaced him. I said nothing to Curley that night. Later he said, "He had me rattled." He never gave any further explanation.

That kind of thing was outside of college. With it there went *séances,* and colloquies with the dead (such as there have been since Adam died) and attempts at thought transference, with doses of Madame Blavatsky and theosophy. A new occult world was growing up like weeds among the tombstones of dead superstitions. *Naturam expellas furco, tamen usque recurrit.*

Then came the Psychical Research Society and the attempt to reduce the occult world to scientific experiment and demonstration. And with that opened new fields of medicine, mind-cure, therapeutics, as old as mind itself but breaking to new life in our own century. Physiology, now better equipped with magnetism and electricity, moved on from Galvani's dead frog with the salt on its leg to delicate experiments that called aloud for new theories of mind and matter. This new medical physiology reached out its hand, and psychology took it, and the dusty old professor in the long gown turned into Psyche the Soul.

. . . .

In other words psychology from being nothing in the curriculum but a humble branch of metaphysics, itself a subdivision of philosophy at large, expanded till it became a whole department, with all kinds of affiliations and extensions, and broke outside the bounds of college to invade life in the open.

. . . .

Psychology has overrun the curriculum by the sheer audacity of its onslaught. It has expanded in all directions at once. It has taken over the dream of the metaphysician and the micrometer of the physiologist. It's an art and it's a science. It's a theory and it's a practice. It's an experiment and a dogma. It is business. It is religion. It has become a regular academic department store with a *Deep Thought Counter, Practical Experiments* in the basement and *Minds Tested Free* near the front door.

In the college which I know best, and, I am sure, in many others, if a benefactor leaves money for a scholarship "in liberal arts," psychology says: "Let me in on that. I'm an art. I'm the biggest dream you ever saw. I'm all thought." If it's for science, psychology says: "Take me in on this. I'm science straight out; look at this testing machine. Stick your brain under it." And if it is a medical gift: "Count me in. Therapeutics is my second name." If it's for theology, psychology slips on a white surplice and points to its courses on the psychology of religion.

Audacity wins. The other subjects stood meekly by and watched psychology take over their fields. To physiology it said: "You take the knife and do the work and I'll make the talk." To economics: "Give me anything your students don't understand about value and demand and I'll fix it so that they don't need to understand it." And to the college at large: "Hand me over the students and I'll test their brains. That's all you need." . . . And it hinted behind its hand, "I can test the professors, too, if you like," and in a lower voice, "What about the President?"

Having conquered the college, psychology turned to business, set up courses in the *Psychology of Business Relations,* and gave lectures at luncheon clubs on the *Psychology of Advertising.* It frightened the business world into submission by threatening it with a course on the *Analytical Measurement of Human Personality,* a thing no business man would want done to himself, though he might like to have it worked on his employees. It let the business man know that it had its eye on him by announcing courses on the *Observation of Social Behaviour,* and it tempted his alliance by hinting at a course on leadership. The business man capitulated, had his employees measured on the *Analytical Plan,* and young women applicants tested by the *Orthogenic Method* instead of by being taken out to lunch.

Then psychology turned to administration and began testing soldiers by asking them to multiply three by three and watching their "reaction" to it. It has invented for us a world of "reactions" and "complexes" and "fixations" and "inhibitions." It has its eye now on the criminal law, for which it aspires to be the star witness, replacing the finger-print expert and the toxicologist and the chemical-solution man by the psychiatrist holding the scales of life and death on whether murder was done as a "fun-impulse" or as part of an "inferiority complex."

.   .   .   .

How much does this whole pretentious claim amount to, and what room is there for psychology in sound education? In my opinion, very little. Put back all that is mere common sense; restore to medicine what is medicine; leave business to business men, and psychology will be back again with nothing but its original mystery and its black gown.

.   .   .   .

Psychology "butts in" on our educational system at the very start. It begins to reduce the world, even of little children, to a maze of "complexes" and "suggestions," "fixations" and "behaviours." Plain right and wrong, common sense, goodness and badness get mixed up in a world that has a terrifying aspect of dark forces working through the individual and not of him. The psychology school child is possessed of new devils, which are working through him to expression. It is not *he* who threw the ink at the teacher; it was a complex that had got inside him. The teacher is not faced with a case of discipline but with a "behaviour problem." She must wipe off the ink and think it out.

Let me quote from a recent educational book, one of a multiplying many:

John F— in school made life miserable for his teacher and also for the other children. He threw erasers across the room. He threw snowballs through the window. He dumped the waste paper all over the

*floor. He erased all the things the teacher had on the
board.*

*The old-fashioned teacher [the author adds] would
say he needed a good thrashing.*

I must confess that it seems to me that the old-
fashioned teacher would not be far wrong. In the days
when I taught school, half a century ago, I think I
could have solved the John F— problem to ten places
of decimals with three feet of bamboo. But it appears
from the text before us that I would have been all
wrong. What John F— needed, we are told, is love.
It was the lack of this that made him throw the erasers
round. He was "expressing himself." What he was
trying to put across was "Love me, or I'll sock you
with this eraser." It is somewhat the same idea as the
Nazis have over in Central Europe.

Why did John F— need love? Because, apparently,
he had picked up a complex, a little sister complex. At
home his little sister Clara had been the family pet and
he hadn't. Who wouldn't sling ink under provocation
like that?

Or consider the psychology of business. This, with
its sub-divisions on salesmanship and such, fills many
courses. Is there any such thing? No, of course not,
or only in the sense in which there is a psychology of
conversation, or psychology of fishing, or of taking a
motor ride, or a psychology of silence.

And salesmanship! Open any of the manuals on it
(I admit they are getting fewer; it has been a flop)

and you will be introduced to a nut called the Prospect. This doesn't mean a landscape; it means the man
to whom you are going to sell something. The nut
called the Prospect doesn't want it, but you are going
to make him take it. You do it partly with your eye
(the nut wilts when you look at him), partly by "suggestion" and partly by "personality." This last attri-
bute will sell anything, but to acquire it you need at
least three hours a week for half a year, and must put
up about a hundred dollars. This salesmanship psychology has invaded our language; people talk now of
"selling an idea"—that is, making it popular. If you
want to get up a club picnic you must get some live
fellow to "sell fresh air"; if you're going to help a
church you'll have to have a group of canvassers to
go and sell religion. The last stage is when you are so
smart that you can sell yourself. They did it in the
Middle Ages and the idea is back again.

The psychology of politics—another piece of nonsense. I knew once a wealthy old Ontario lumber-man
who said, "If any man can change his politics after an
election quicker than I can, I want to see him." You
can, if you like, make a book of that sort of thing;
but you don't need four hours a week, four months a
year (Mon., Tues., Thurs., Sat.) to understand it.

.   .   .   .

With that go the psychology tests and question-
naires:

*As our firm has an application from Mr. William
Worm for a job as a calliper, will you kindly give your*

*confidential) opinion as to his (1) Personality (2)
Malleability (3) Obesity (4) Mortality. . . .*

In reply to which the Department of Psychology
assigns to William Worm his proper percentage in
each.

.   .   .   .

The pychologist, in other words, has managed so to
impose himself on the world that he is now "called
in" in a difficulty, like an emergency plumber. When
he takes the final step of being "Open Day and
Night," his status will be complete. Meantime, as far
as we are concerned with a curriculum for people who
don't want to lose a year of life over the futilities of
behaviour and will take their chance on personality,
psychology should be put back to where it was.

But we're all afraid of it. It might put a curse on
us, or an inhibition.

VIII

Teaching the Unteachable

CHAPTER VIII

TEACHING THE UNTEACHABLE

The barnacles on the academic ship: Fake courses for
he feeble-minded: Clothing Analysis, Dry Skiing and
he Theory of Girls' Sports as College Courses; Peda-
jogy and a year's loss of life; Teaching Business; the
Lotus Land of Idle Talk

N my opinion the great majority of the colleges of
he United States and Canada contain in their cur-
iculums of liberal arts an accumulation of courses
vhich are little more than an attempt to teach the un-
eachable; which substitute for the rigour of real study
a make-believe activity and a dilettante idleness; which
ry to make theory out of the commonplace and to
urn the obvious into the intricate; which are as pre-
entious as they are futile and which in the extreme
ases are the mere bogus coin of academic currency.

These courses are carried along as a dead weight,
ike the barnacles that gather on the bottom of a sail-
ng ship. The only purpose that they serve is to enable
oung people to come to college who could never have
lone so in the sterner days of the old-time curriculum
—young men who can study tap dancing and social
behaviour but not Latin and physics; young women
vho can't learn algebra but can manage archery; and
oung people of both sexes whose minds are nicely

fitted to a course on the *Theory and Practice of Bad-minton,* or a course on *Marriage,* open only to seniors and pursued intensively in the spring quarter.

I cannot speak of what the situation is in Great Britain, but I am inclined to think that at any rate the newer British colleges have to some extent followed our false lead. Nor am I speaking here of the purely technical schools of medicine and applied science. I am certain that they have enough real subjects of study, of increasing interest and intensity, to make it unneces-sary to fake up false ones. I am talking here of the schools of liberal arts and the associated schools of social science, commerce, education, journalism, and home economics which have invaded and overrun its territory.

The result is deplorable. Much of our study is turn-ing to mere wool-gathering, to pretentious nonsense. The rigour of it is melting away like butter. A lot of it is so easy, so vague and so silly that anything nicely above an athropoid ape can get a degree in it.

What are we to say, for example, to a course on *Clothing Analysis,* which the college curriculum says is "designed to create in the student an enthusiasm for possessing individuality in clothes"? What an awaken-ing of genius must this course occasion! One imagines some young inspired dreamer, waking in the night and leaping from his couch to seize a piece of chalk and sketch out an idea for the shape of his pants. Gradu-ates returning to the farm with a gold medal for indi-viduality in clothes would be pretty expensive to keep Yet the course is given in a university with an hon oured name and a hundred years of history.

Let us set beside it, from the program of one of the largest of the State universities, a course in *Kinesiology*. What this is, I don't know. I never got as far as that in Greek. But the context shows that it is for men only, and the derivation seems to indicate that it is for fast men, or perhaps for men who need speeding up. They get it three times a week—right after lunch. It must be a great strain.

And here, taken from the curriculum of a great Pacific institution, but findable in many other colleges, is an *Introduction to Religion*. Most of us got that at our mother's knee. But these people get it every Tuesday and Thursday at eleven. The danger would be that they might go all to the devil by Monday night.

In the same college is a department of Physical Education for women which has among other things a set of "activities" courses. These include *Dry Skiing*, which ought to call for a balancing course in *Wet Golf*. In the list also appears "life-saving," a thing which, in my day, students left to the bartender at seven o'clock the next morning. But these people evidently have a good time all the time; they do tennis, sailing, archery, tap dancing and wind up with tumbling. It is only fair to add that various colleges list tap dancing and archery, and one has the hardihood to announce a course on the *Fundamentals of Golf for Beginners*. One can imagine the boy who is taking the individual study in pants going out in plus fours to get his fundament in golf.

Even there the academic sin is not so unpardonable

as in the creation of courses with made-up names that are a mere burlesque of scholarship such as *Kinesiology*. Put beside it, as drawing cards, taken from the 1939 calendars of various colleges, the courses in *Eurambics,* in *Choric Speaking,* and *Human Ecology.* This last sounds like being sick. But apparently there are students today prepared to take a course on anything with a name with a proper sound, such as *Rheumatics, Spondulics* or *Peritonitis.*

The courses I have cited above are all actual. Indeed, everything said in this chapter about these newer studies is based on an examination of the latest program of study issued by fifty American Universities, selected among the best known, among the largest and the most characteristic. I did not include any institutions of a purely freakish character. The examples that I have cited can be duplicated over and over again till even the fun squeezes dry out of them and leaves nothing but the fraud and the shame. Nor do I know of any university in the United States or Canada entirely free from this sloppy degeneration. Seven of them, Toronto, Chicago, Brown, Dartmouth, Queen's, Bishop's and McGill, I have the right to call my Alma Mater—either a mother under whose care I studied or at least as the wet-nurse of an honorary degree. But not even my gratitude toward these institutions can lead me to deny that they have gone astray in the wilderness with their sister colleges. Nor is this, I think, the mere complaint of an old man—*Laudator temporis acti*—to whom the grass was green and the sky blue fifty years ago. Some things that old men think might be true, even in this age of Youth.

. . . .

All this false attempt to teach the unteachable has grown up in the last fifty years. When faith in the older classical curriculum began to weaken in a new world of science and industry, it seemed proper to expand the studies of a college to meet the expanding needs of the hour. The original motive was at least sound and praiseworthy. The idea was to make the college *practical,* to harmonize it with a practical world, to bring the college to the student and to teach him the things on which his livelihood would depend. A classical scholar of the older type began to appear singularly inept. He didn't know how to drive a motor-car, or put a washer on a kitchen tap, or go down to the cellar to replace an electric fuse. For things like this you had to get "a man." The classical scholar couldn't go near the Stock Exchange unless a trustee held him by the hand, couldn't read a balance sheet and didn't know what F.O.B. meant. A mathematician was about as bad, useful to make insurance tables and the nautical almanac, but no personality, no magnetism. What the world began to need was "dynamos," "live-wires," "executives."

So a new stream of studies began to flow into liberal arts—at first as a leak in the classical dam, then as a flood that swept the dam away and left only a few fragments of it as islands in the new water.

Political economy came first, highly respectable, with credentials from Adam Smith and John Stuart Mill.

After it came sociology, a sort of windy first cousin to religion, with a letter of recommendation from Herbert Spencer. Then came education, hitherto only practice but turned now to a theory and a discipline, which not only invaded college, but set up a college of its own. Schools of commerce sprang up and flourished on the aid of business men, flattered by being automatically turned into a profession. There was now the same fervour to break away from Latin as with the Protestants to break away from Rome. With commerce came journalism and physical education, by which high jumping and skinning-the-cat were turned into theory, and home economics whereby such things as cooking, marketing and nursing the baby were dressed up as college courses, as African natives dress up in plug hats and soda water bottles on string.

In all these changes there is of course a certain modicum of reason, of sensible adaptation of older study to newer life. But the essential point is that the practical goal which they propose to reach cannot be reached by that road. Education, in the sense of the power to teach, is learned by becoming a teacher; commerce is learned in an office or a warehouse, and banking in a bank. Journalism is learned in a newspaper office and nursing the baby is learned by getting married.

College is meant to train the mind, not the thumb. A certain modicum of discussion and attention can be given in pauses of the sterner studies to such things as lectures on society at large (sociology) or to the theory of how best to learn and to teach (education).

But these things as they stand are exalted and expanded out of all proportion to their usefulness. When a student turns his whole course into journalism it is as if he proposed to make his whole diet on sugar. If a student having had an *Introduction to Religion* goes ahead and takes ten more courses in it, I doubt if he is getting much nearer to the Kingdom of Heaven. If religion is what I think it is—a communing of the spirit with the unseen, an imminent sense of life beyond death and of duty laid upon us—I don't see how you can take a "course" in it, unless you don't believe in it. Human life itself is the only course in religion. What colleges call "comparative religion" would have seemed, in an age of belief, rank blasphemy.

Consider education. By this is meant not the body of knowledge itself, but the manner and mechanism of imparting it. Schools of education constantly forget this little distinction, and keep themselves well nourished by stealing over the fence. Kept within its own fields, the diet is pretty scanty. The notion that a student must spend one fifth of all his college life, one fifth of all his parents' college money in learning how to teach the things he has learned already (four years arts, one year pedagogy) is just a sham and a fraud. If the idea is only designed to help keep the teaching profession closed, to help keep up the market, let us do it some other way, as they do in France with the closed shop called the Aggregation. But the pretence that "pedagogy" is worth a year of life is wicked.

I have a certificate in the stuff dating back to 1888.

In those happy days we escaped with a three months'
sentence. I put in my time, aged eighteen, at the old
Collegiate Institute of Strathroy, Ontario, and had
among the pupils on whom I practiced General Sir
Arthur Currie, then a boy of thirteen just entering
high school. We had to study a book or two on the
history of education, interesting enough, but as easy
as mud pie to anyone trained on Greek and mathematics. We studied also a text or two on the theory
of education, all of it as obvious as coming in out of
the wet. We were taught that education must proceed
from the concrete to the abstract, from the known to
the unknown, and so forth.

In later life, with forty-six years of teaching, I have
realized that, obvious as it is, a lot of this isn't so. It
is often very good business as a short cut to begin with
something abstract and unknown, and for the moment
unintelligible, and later come out into the sunlight of
understanding. It is like going through a tunnel under
a hill instead of wandering miles round it. All the side
issues that are taught in education courses, such as
school ventilation and the care of the teeth, should be
left to a plumber or a doctor. Beyond these again are
the excrescences, such things as a course on the list in
front of me, called *Field Practice in Guidance and
Counselling*. These are just sin against the light.

Education, as theory in a general sense, is interesting to read about and to think about. Like sociology
it is fit reading for old men. But it isn't a college
course. Education, as practice, begins when you really
start to teach, as I did in Uxbridge High School on a

February morning in 1889. All that Strathroy had
done for me was to break the ice; the plunge had still
to come. A couple of months' initiation into practical
teaching, taken while still in the arts course, is all that
any teacher can ever need or benefit by. To steal a
year of youth is robbery. One recalls how Emile Zola
in the Dreyfus case kept repeating *J'accuse!* That is
how I feel. *J'accuse* Pedagogy.

Now hand me down commerce. We'll take it on
next. It is wholly impossible to teach "business" in a
school or college. You can teach certain things useful
as a training for an intelligent business man, such as
how to read and write well, and express himself properly. In this, Latin is excellent, and enough mathematics to heighten his power of concentration. And along-
side of his real education you can, if he wishes, give
him a knowledge of book-keeping, though few business
men know anything about it; and company organization, which most people leave to lawyers; and short-
hand and typing, usually bought by the week. But the
main part of the education of a business man is not to
fit him for his business but to fit him to live. If a boy
is to be trained for the coal and wood business, just
for that, with no life apart from it and no soul, then
he needs no college and college has nothing for him.
Rub coal-dust on his face and put him to work at four-
teen. Don't cheat him into taking a six months' credit
on the *Theory of Nut Coal*.

The subject of journalism occupies an enormous
space in the newer college curriculum, especially in certain universities in the Middle West. In more than one

of them the courses number as many as forty, and
would occupy, if taken as a total, several years of a
student's life. They range from such obvious things as
the *History of Journalism* to special courses on writing editorials, city reporting, small town newspapers.
One large institution situated among the oil wells offers a special course on reporting gas and oil, including, no doubt, explosions, a subject needing apparently
an intensive training in lurid language.

Now anyone whose activity in life, in whole or in
part, consists of writing must feel a certain sympathy
with the attempt to bring college training to the aid
of a prospective writer. That the college can be of
enormous use to a young man who wants to be a journalist there is no doubt. But essentially what such a
person needs is English—both literature and composition—and history with a special view of our contemporary era and our current government and a certain
training in one or more modern languages, with Latin
always as the background. In science he needs what is
elsewhere described in the book as a "thorough smattering." In other words a journalist must be a man
with a wide education and a ready knowledge of the
world in which we live. Such subjects as proof-reading
and make-up and the handling of dispatches can be
learned in a newspaper office, and can't be learned
anywhere else.

The notion that there is a special training in English
needed for writing editorials and another for writing
obituaries and another for writing up local items is not
only erroneous but injurious. A person who writes for

a newspaper very soon learns certain tricks of the
trade, arising out of necessity. Thus he must learn to
call a murderer an alleged murderer, and the King
of England the alleged King of England. This fore-
stalls libel suits. In writing up local events he must
learn to state what happened, the whole of it, in one
long breathless sentence, called a "lead," at the very
start, so that the reader need go no further. He must
learn to avoid personalities and give the sources of his
information as coming from "a leading oil interest,"
or from "rubber circles," or "a reliable pulp and paper
source." In this immaterialized world of oil and rubber and pulp there is no fear of offence. But even when
a journalist has become familiar with all these tricks
and tags, the question still remains, can he write? And
for this there is no royal academic road, and an alleged training in alleged journalism, if it cuts the student out from a proper share in wider, deeper culture,
is dearly bought.

Other subjects again, such as sociology, are excellent
things in their way but have not sufficient body, defi-
niteness or order in them to make them a subject of
curriculum study. They represent reflection, not training. Take out of sociology all that is history or belongs with such anterior studies as geology, palaeontology, and anthropology, and what is left? Nothing
but general speculation that expresses itself in the announced courses in such forms as *"Social Trends,* a
study of the factors and forces involved in the organization and continual modification of society." Now you
can't take a boy off a farm and teach him a social

trend, at the rate of four hours of trend per week, ending up with one credit in *Social Trends*. A wise old man like Plato or a wise young man like Herbert Spencer might muse on the topic and write on it, and other wise people might read it and enjoy it and profit by it. But you can't *teach* it. It isn't college.

If all this pleasant dilettante discussion, this mimic make-believe could be had for nothing, if it did not involve the loss of time and money and opportunity, it would not matter. In a world where it was always afternoon young men and women might sit among the lotus leaves, or in the shade of the catalpas and talk of "social trends" and "personnel psychology" till they nodded off asleep. In the world as it is there is no room for such a slumber, for such a sleep, for such a folding of the hands to sleep. We have it on authority what may happen next.

IX

Rah! Rah! College!

CHAPTER IX
RAH! RAH! COLLEGE!

Niggers in a compound — The college that was; oat-meal and anatomy — The college that is: Co-eds and snap courses — The charm of college life — College activities — Pep Clubs and Poultry Clubs — Student executives — The fortunate few — Education that never dies

I REMEMBER noting, when I was in South Africa thirty years ago, how certain great mines on the Rand were shut in as compounds with tall metal fences, so that the Portuguese East African "niggers" working in the mine might be persuaded to stay on the job. When they came up from under the earth, in the pauses of their labour, there arose in the compound the sound of music and the banjo and the loud laughter that marked the African's appreciation of the vaudeville troupe hired to entertain him. It was not philanthropy that led the mining companies to entertain the niggers with vaudeville, and to drive away their sorrows with the banjo. Without that, the niggers wouldn't work, would pine away and die. It was hard enough to get them there anyway. Nothing did it but the prospect of getting out a couple of years later, with money enough to go home and buy two wives and a spy glass and a case of gin. That was their graduation day.

. . . .

The students in our colleges are the niggers in the compound. From inside the college fence rises the sound of "Rah! Rah! College!" as they carry on their student activities which correspond to the nigger's vaudeville! Listen! You can hear the Banjo and Mandolin Club practising in Convocation Hall for the big show tomorrow night put on by the United Sororities League in honour of the big victory at the big game on Saturday. Most of the profs have cancelled their lectures this afternoon to get ready for the holiday tomorrow. You can't hold a class the day before a holiday. A class is as delicate to "hold," anyway, as the bubble in a spirit level. Listen again! In the pauses of the banjo and mandolin you can hear the Rooters Club, away across the campus in the gym practising their cheers for tomorrow. "Prexy" himself let them off classes today to practise, but he said he wanted the cheers to be clean and spontaneous. Well—as the Rooters' cheer leader said—you can't get a spontaneous cheer without spade work. That's it—spade work. There's a lot of it going on all round, in the buildings and in the campus. Committees are meeting to do spade work on the program of welcome, and inside groups are doing spade work to get the committees into line. Bright, busy—such a happy scene, all autumn leaves and colour.

Such a happy place is college, made so by the college activities that serve as the niggers' vaudeville of the students. If it were not so, how could the students reconcile themselves to the long ten years of prepara tion for life that they must face in coming in, and pay off year by year—in years counted out one by one—their promissory note discounted on the future.

In earlier days this was not so. College was short and stern; it was like a prayer before a battle, in the days when one year in a saw-mill and two years in a winter class made a doctor, there was not time for college activities. The banjo—or was it the bagpipes?—hung silent on the student's wall. The Edinburgh "medico" ate his oatmeal and counted his anatomy bones, grim and determined. But his eye was on the promised land.

.   .   .   .

Few people realize how agreeable is college life, how halcyon its days, and how stern and rugged it has been elsewhere and in other days. Not, of course, always so; there have been times and places in the past where college life meant little more than wine and cards, driving in "drags" and having "rags" and keeping it up till one was sent down. Here and there, undisturbed by the rags, classical dons annotated Greek texts, or the individual studies of an Adam Smith or an Edward Gibbon redeemed the torpor of the mass.

But in most places, sixty years or so ago, in Scotland and on this continent at least, college life was stern, its studies a veritable sentence to hard labour. Take this for example, a reminiscence of the late Sir James Barrie, as evidence of the student life in Edinburgh as it once was.

"*I knew three undergraduates,*" *said Barrie,* "*who lodged together in one room in a dreary house at the top of a dreary street. Two of them used to study till two in the morning while the third slept. When they shut up their books they woke No. 3 who studied till breakfast time. Among the advantages of the arrangement the chief was that, as they were dreadfully poor, one bed did for three. Two of them occupied it at one time and one at another.*"

There is nothing attractive in such a picture; little in it but a shudder, with a certain admiration of the staying power that could stick it out. But it represents one extreme of which "college activity" of today is the other. The Scottish student overdid his poverty. He could have worked a year for wages—he had at least a year of life to trade—and changed his penury to relative affluence. Thus have I seen students of the Middle West working their way through college with long hours of menial labour as the price of study. Their case, in a way, is worse than the lot of the Scot, since our long curriculum makes it hard to add on a year. Nor could anyone wish college life back to where it was, with so little diversion, so rigorous in its work, so cut off from the society of the other sex, life's solace and life's danger—cut off as a dead sea, stormless in a chasm.

.   .   .   .

All different is the picture of college life now. Only those of us who have lived in college—not merely studied there for four years; that's nothing, but *lived* there—can fully tell of the charm and amenity of college life. The college years pass by, from autumn leaves to autumn leaves, in a measured cadence that substitutes the college calendar for the Zodiac. Here are the seasons all reversed and defied, where autumn is springtime, bright and eager with the hopes of a new college year, where December is the very noontime of effort and activity, and so onward, till the fading year melts into spring and vanishes with the flowers of June.

Little do we note the flight of time, as the college, itself immortal, drifts toward eternity. What to us is weather or the storm? We have our lighted classroom, and the February snow outside the window can but render it more inviting—the professor at his desk, expounding, for the thirtieth winter, his notes on Kant's estimate of Aristotle's view of Plato, and the class, their heads bent over their desks, writing it all diligently down—as their fathers and mothers did thirty years ago, when the prof was a sessional lecturer and wore a flower in his coat and worked each night to have the next day's lecture ready, as busy as a baker making bread.

That's the life, the college life, of the class-room, and of the outside "college activities" for which the class-room serves as a pleasant recuperation.

. . . .

I know no more attractive scene than the campus of a college on the autumn day when the students gather for the new session—the commencement of another academic year. The sky is never so blue nor

the still, fleecy clouds so white, nor the autumn leaves
so bright with red and russet and yellow, as on that
day.

Bright as they are their colours are dimmed beside
the reds and whites of the college blazers of the co-
eds, grouped with their fellow students in happy greet-
ings and reunions under the trees, or moving about as
busy and as aimless as an ant-hill. Here and there
moves also a "prof," a queer mixture of summer tan
and academic dinginess, to lend a contrast of age to
this surrounding world of youth.

Inside the halls all is crowding and jostling, activity
and eagerness and laughter. The students are trying to
register and can't, and so they stand waiting in long
queues outside the offices of Deans and Women's Su-
pervisors. No college ever manages a system of regis-
tration that works; each *has* one, a marvel of theory,
invented by Professor Angle (see under *Department
of Psychology*) fifteen years ago and as out of date as
the professor himself.

But the students don't mind. They wait endlessly
bandied about from Dean to Dean, from Supervisor
to Supervisor, or falling into talk and breaking off to
shout a greeting to Bill, the janitor of Liberal Arts, the
only efficient man in the university.

The students, of course, are concerned with their
courses, their "elections" and their "options"—what
they are to take for the coming session. It's like the
babble of a stock-market. Professor Dim is said to be
offering a new course in *Greek Archaeology;* very few
takers; it's rumoured that he ploughed a student last

year. There's a big rush for *English Seventeen,* the Drama, but the prof has a notice up that he won't let in any more—still you might try to see him in his office. There's the usual mob for *Sociology One,* and there are three students, so they say, in *Fourth Year Honour Mathematics,* where there have been none for five years.

Here in one of the groups is a pretty girl in a college blazer, cursing, with a happy oath that wouldn't take the skin off a peach, at the Dean of Women, because the old cat won't let her elect *Religion;* says she hasn't the prerequisite. And she swears she has—really swears.

Here are a couple of football men gravely discussing with a junior prof, himself an ex-quarter-back, what they had better take. *Archaeology* looks likely, as the lecturer never takes the roll and no one has failed in it within memory, but there's a new course on *Delinquency,* under psychology, that is better, because it has no prerequisite, no roll-call, attendance left to student's honour and the credit is given on the professor's own say so.

. . . .

But of course more than all, most of all, the students are discussing the clubs and societies and activities. Who's to be editor of the *Daily Hoot?* What freshmen are being canvassed for the fraternities— the *Oh, Few, Few,* and the *Mew, Mew Fie* and so on. There's a general notice of the first meeting of the Glee Club, all up! and the organizing meeting of the Discussion Club, all up! and the first lunch of the

Dutch Treat (basement of the cafeteria), all down!

And so, endlessly and happily. If life offers any collective thing better than this day, which I have seen come and go more than forty times, then I've missed it.

.   .   .   .

Such is college activity. But, as with all good things, the only question is, how far do you go with it? A wise old Greek once took as his life motto, *Do nothing too much;* and I remember a similar case in point when the town council of my home town, in pensioning an old employee, made the pension "for life, but not more than five years." So with the activities. If education is eating up life is it not possible that "activity" is eating up education?

The difficulty about the students' activities and the clubs and societies under which they are organized is that every one of them—or nearly every one of them —taken by itself, seems not only justifiable but admirable. A Literary and Debating Society—excellent! What college could be without it? A Glee Club! Why shouldn't a student sing, just as why shouldn't a soldier drink? A Dramatic Society, A Cercle Français to talk real French, a Deutscher Bund to eat pretzels! Fine.

Even when the list gets a little doubtful we can perhaps turn an indulgent eye, as upon a good idea gone astray. Here, for example, is a Pep Club—not in one college but in several. The purpose of it is defined by one of the colleges in its calendar by saying, "This club is composed of young women who are associated for the purpose of generating enthusiasm

for inter-collegiate athletic contests." One thinks of
Helen of Troy, whose face launched a thousand ships,
and shudders to think of the dangers into which the
Pep Club may plunge the fated boys. In one college
the Pep Club has an offshoot, the "Green Peppers,"
under the supervision of the Pep Club. This is composed of "freshman girls," and is prepared to make
trouble by generating enthusiasm among school-boys.
. . Odd, isn't it, that the underlying idea of so many
of these societies is that you can't get enthusiasm unless you generate it, can't hold, can't feel anything
till you wave your arms. . . . You must go into life
body first and drag your head in afterwards. But perhaps it is only part of "mass method" on which we
now live. . . .

Here is another college with a Poultry Club and a
Dairy Club that sound as warm and friendly as a
barn-yard but are offset by a Cosmopolitan Club that
wouldn't know a cow from an antelope. Compare with
these peaceful activities the Scabbard and Blade organization, an honorary military fraternity of various
colleges, prepared to demolish the enemies of its country either seriatim or in the mass. Put beside it the
Quadrangle Club, a "religious society" whose purpose
is the "development of the four-square man" or, so
to say, the man of four dimensions—"spiritual, mental, physical and social." Presumably he is hard to de-
velop and needs isolation in a club, like a bacillus in
a culture.

The parent source of all was, I imagine, the old-
time Literary and Debating Society. Pretty dim its

meetings were. In the one I remember best the college
rule forbade all debate that touched on religion, politics or contemporary affairs. The usual topic was one
such as "Resolved that the execution of Charles the
First was justified." Charles had his head resolved
on and off him at a hundred college sessions.

Beside this went the College Glee Club, as natural
and as mournful as lost Tasmanians singing on a rock.
On the side, of course, were the Greek Letter Societies
that are not under discussion here. In colleges without
resident life they were one thing; in colleges equipped
with dormitories and furnished with three hundred social activities they are another.

With the Debating Society and the Glee Club was
the original College Journal, appearing about once a
month, more or less, in a sort of arctic twilight, discussing "The Genius of Shakespeare," "An Autumn
Walk," with Latin verses, *"Tu, Tulle, tute meo,"* etc.
No one followed it further.

The change came in a rising tide that turned to a
tidal wave. The newer subjects, political economy
and such, started "clubs" which compelled the old
ones to break out in the same spot—the History Club,
the Philosophy Club, the Physics Club, right back to
Bible Clubs and Old Testament Societies that scored
a bull's-eye on creation. All, be it noted, were excellent
in idea. Then the old *College Journal* expanded into
the new *College Daily,* with editorial rooms, reporters,
everything up to murder. With it came subsidiary
sheets and organs. The Glee Club extended into musical societies, choral societies, folk song societies, and,

est of all, gave birth to the Dramatic Society, the
most justifiable of all college institutions, except of
course the Old Testament Club. The work done by
dramatic societies, making and producing plays, is real
education, with the true prompting of spontaneous interest that is lost elsewhere. It is not based on the
mere "camp-meeting" enthusiasm of the "Let's all
shout" organizations.

Side by side with these grew up another set of organizations to remind the student of his home—in the
Eastern universities, Western Clubs and in the Western universities, Eastern Clubs, and everywhere, in
Canada at least, Maritime Province Clubs, because
everybody comes from the Maritime Provinces, and
nobody goes there.

.   .   .   .

The names of the clubs and societies, if you put
them all together, is legion. One of the largest of the
State universities writes proudly of itself, "Practically
every type of American college student organization
is found among the three hundred clubs, societies and
associations represented upon the University campus."

.   .   .   .

There would be no great harm done if each one
student followed only one activity; if he staggered
home late from his chess club but was at his books
early in the morning; if he blew his whole face into
his trombone from four to six but was at his desk in
the evening; if he wrote a brilliant article on "The
World's Awakening," in the *Student's Daily* and then
fell asleep over his trigonometry.

But it is not so. Even the average student follow half a dozen activities, and all the most efficient an capable are so immersed in them that they turn int executives and committee men, with their day full, n time to turn round. Capable indeed they are—fa quicker of comprehension than real business men, wit more enthusiasm and more precision in their mind They need to have enthusiasm and energy, too, fo there are so many activities to be kept going that th leaders must do a terrific lot of organizing, initiating committee work, spade work, to keep the others u to it. All up! for this, and all up! for that, till colleg life becomes a sort of permanent "resurrection day." And for such a day, spade work is the first requisite.

One recalls how a famous French general looked o at the charge of the Light Brigade at Balaclava an said, "It's magnificent but it isn't war." So with thes student leaders—it's wonderful but it isn't study. I is making of them fine and efficient men and women But the toll of years taken is too heavy, and the lif of the college, as they lead it, would never keep aligh the lamp of learning.

.   .   .   .

But there are those who trim it.

Here and there in this moving and happy worl there are among the students the few who leaven th lump, the few who really study. You remember ho Edgar Allan Poe said, "And the people, ah, the peo ple, they that live up in the steeple." Well, there ar students up in the steeple of the temple of learning or higher still, up in the clouds. These are the one who come to college and never go away, whose lot it is, thrice blessed, to stay at college all their lives—demonstrating first, and then lecturing, and then moved up to be an associate, and later on a professor, a real one. Somewhere in such a professor's life he has picked up, more or less unnoticed, a wife, as a beaver picks up a mate away off in the woods. Married or single it makes but little difference; life flows on from session to session, smooth and unruffled as seen by the outside eye, but, as seen from within, full of its eager struggles, its triumphs and its landmarks. Such is, for instance, the occasion when the professor reads his first paper (all typed by his wife) before the Palaeontological Society, or has his article on the "Diphthongs in Chaucer" accepted by the *Philomathic Journal*.

For these people, study is study; its foundation is laid deep and its crown is never set. For their sake I gladly take back everything said in this book, of shorter methods, fewer declensions and less exceptions. They need them all. No "smattering" for them. When they tackle an author they dissect him from the head down and hang up the skin. They follow the tide of human thought from Plato downward till they almost, never quite, reach yesterday. Each carries with him his life work, like that of Professor Dim with the *Odyssey* described elsewhere in this book. And his life work—on the geography of Ninevah or the place names of Yucatan or the coleoptera of the British Isles—is seldom complete, usually but a fragment and often never begun. They need time, these men; they need eternity. Collectively they get it, and the college goes on, maintained, as far as its soul is concerned, by the men who work in it, and not by the bricks and mortar that house their labours.

I have written elsewhere that, with the right men and a few elm trees and some books, one could have, at a generation's notice, the most distinguished college in the world. I repeat it here so that the animating idea of this book may not be obscured. This is not a plea for cheaper, shorter education in the mean sense, but for education that does not end with college and for learning that never dies. Rah! Rah! College! Let's go and see what's happening in the campus.

KINDRED ESSAYS IN EDUCATION
AND HUMOUR

When Men Retire

WHEN MEN RETIRE

My old friend Mr. McPherson retired from the flour and feed business—oh, quite a few years ago. He said it was time to get out and give young Charlie a chance—even then "young Charlie" was getting near fifty. Anyway old Mr. McPherson said he wasn't going to keep his nose to the grindstone for ever.

I don't mean that he absolutely dropped out of the business; but, as he himself said, he took it easy. The McPhersons had a fine business, two or three big mills and a central office in our home town. Always, before he retired, Mr. McPherson would be down at the office sharp at eight—t'; flour and feed is an early business. When he retired he gave all that up. He'd loaf in anywhere round ten minutes past, or sometimes even twenty. It was the same way after lunch—or at least I mean after "dinner"; they don't have "lunch" in the flour and feed business; they have dinner at noon. After dinner if Mr. McPherson didn't feel like getting up and walking to the office at one o'clock, he'd drive down in a cab. And at five o'clock, when the office closed, if he didn't feel like going home right away, he'd stay for a while and run over some of the day's invoices. Or perhaps, if he felt like it, he'd go over to the mill, because the mill didn't close till six, and just fool around there a while helping the men bag up some of the farmers' orders.

One thing, though, that Mr. McPherson insists on,

now that he's retired, is that, as he himself says, he never interferes. The business, as he explains, belongs now to the children. That means young Charlie and Lavinia—bless me! Lavinia must be not far from sixty; she keeps the house. To those two and a married daughter in Scotland. The old man has never transferred the business in any legal sense. He says it isn't necessary as long as he's alive. But it's *theirs* just the same, and he tells them so. And, as I say, he doesn't interfere; "young Charlie" is the general manager, and all his father does is just to look over the contracts to see what's doing, and keep an eye on the produce market to advise young Charlie when to buy—but only, mind you, to advise.

What's more, as Mr. McPherson himself loves to explain, he's not like a man who can't cut loose from business and enjoy himself. Oh, my no! Every year there's the St. Andrews dinner in the Odd Fellows' Hall, regular as clock-work, and every year Burns' birthday, when a few of them get together and have a big old time and read Burns out loud. And only four years ago Mr. McPherson took a trip to Scotland and saw his married daughter and Burns' grave and the big flour mills at Dumbarton, and paid for it all out of a commission on No. 1 wheat. Oh, no, Mr. McPherson says he never regrets his retirement: he can't think what it would be like to be back in harness.

     .   .   .   .

My friend McAlpin was a banker—assistant general manager of a bank. He retired in the natural, normal course of things in accordance with the bank regulations. He made no plan or preparation for retirement. He said that it was enough for him to be rid of the strain of work. He'd have his mind free. So he would have had, if it hadn't happened that, on his first morning of retirement, as he walked down town, he felt a sort of wheeziness, a kind of, well, not exactly a pain, but a sort of compression. Anyway, a druggist gave him some bicarbonate of bismuth—he's told me about it himself ever so many times—or was it bisulphate of something? Anyway it fixed McAlpin up all right but it left him with a sort of feeling of flatulence, or flobbulence (he's explained it to me) that bothered him all morning till a friend told him to drink Vichy water, two or three quarts at a time. Now as a matter of fact you see, McAlpin had had that wheeziness every morning for years back when he went to the bank. But as soon as he opened the mail and began dictating, the wheeziness vanished, and the flobbulence never started. But the moment he retired, the wheeziness brought on the flobbulence; and Vichy water is all right, but there's so much chalk in it that if you take it you must follow it with an anticalcide of some sort. I don't know the names, but McAlpin has told me about them—bigusphate of carbon or any other antiscorbutic.

In fact, as McAlpin tells me, he has come to realize that his diet while he was in the bank was all wrong. He used to take bacon and eggs for breakfast, whereas now that he has looked into things he finds that bacon has no food value at all—contains no postulates. Eggs would be all right if taken with a germicide, but they lack vitamins. So what McAlpin eats now—he tells me this himself—is a proper balance of protein and carbohydrates.

McAlpin spends a good deal of his time in the drug stores. He says those follows know a lot. Do you realize that if you take a drink of mineral water every half hour, with a touch of salt in it, it keeps your sebaceous glands open?

When McAlpin takes a holiday he goes down to Nugget Springs where the thermal baths are. It's a new place and he says that they say that the doctors say that the water has a lower alkali content than any other. That's why he goes there, for the low alkali content. You take a bath every hour and in between you drink the water and the rest of the time you sit in it. McAlpin says that when he comes back he feels a hundred per cent more crustaceous than he did before. He attributes this to phosphorus.

.   .   .   .

My friend Tharpe, who was in Iron and Steel, retired to Paris. He retired at fifty-eight. He said he wanted to retire while he was still fresh enough to enjoy life—feel those muscles. He wanted to have a little fun in life, before he sank into old age. So he went over to Paris to have, as he himself so fervently put it, "a whale of a time."

I saw him there six months later, in a night-supper restaurant. He had with him something that looked like an odelisk—isn't that the word?—anyway something Moorish with slanting eyes and a crescent diadem. Tharpe came over and spoke to me. He looked like a boiled lobster, all red and black. He said he felt fine. He said he was just starting out for the evening. He felt, he said, A.1.

I saw him in the hotel next morning. He was in the barber shop. The barber was fixing him up. He looked about four colors, mostly black and yellow. He said he felt great. The barber was steaming him, boiling him and squirting things over him. Then he went up to the drug store and the druggist "fixed him"— washed him right out—and then into the bar and the bartender "fixed him"—toned him right up with a couple of "eye-openers." Then he started off. He had on a pongee suit and a panama hat and a French silk tie, and he looked pretty slick, but battered. He said he felt fine. He said he was going out to play baccarat with two men he met the night before—Russians— he couldn't remember their names—Sonovitch or Dombroski or something. Anyway one of them was a cousin of the Czar. He said he felt elegant.

Tharpe is in a home just now, in England—a rest home. He's taking the rest cure, and then he is to take the gold cure and after that a brain cure. A big English doctor took out part of his skull. He says he feels A.1. He has lost most of his money and he's coming back to the Iron and Steel business. He says it beats Paris.

. . . .

A peculiarly interesting case of retirement has been that of my long-time friend the Senior Professor of

Greek at the college here. When he retired the Chancellor of the University said at the Convocation that our regret at Professor Dim's retirement was tempered by the fact that we realized that he would now be able to complete the studies on Homer's *Odyssey* which had occupied him for so many years. Notice, to *complete*. The general supposition was that in all these long years, in all the evenings of his spare time he'd been working on Homer's *Odyssey,* and that now all that he needed was a little time and breathing space and the brilliant studies would be consolidated into a book. To *complete*—and I was the only one who knew that he hadn't even started. He had begun, ever so many years ago, when we were fellow juniors, talking of Homer's *Odyssey*. There was something he wanted to do about it—I forget just what; either to prove that there was never any Homer or that there was never any Odyssey. At any rate it was one of those big academic problems that professors select as a life work. It began to be understood that he was "working on Homer's *Odyssey*"; then that he was doing a book on Homer's *Odyssey,* and then that he had nearly done it, and only needed time to *complete* it. And all the time he hadn't started. Professors are like that.

· · · · · · ·

The years go by so easily—Commencement Day and a new session—you can't begin anything then—mid-session, impossible—final exams and the end of the session—out of the question to start anything then; a man must rest sometime. And you don't start Homer in the long vacation on the coast of Maine.

So when Professor Dim retired, people on the street would stop him and ask, "How's the book coming on?" And he could only turn pink and gurgle something. I'm the only one who knows that he hasn't started it. He's been getting pretty frail the last two winters; some of his old pupils sent him south last winter, so that he could finish his book. He didn't. They gave him a trip up north last summer—but not far enough. They talk now of sending him to Greece where the *Odyssey* began. They're afraid, some of them—this, of course, they say very gently and kindly —they're afraid that the old fellow may not live to finish the book. I know that he won't. He hasn't started.

But as to this retirement business, let me give a word of advice to all of you young fellows round fifty. Some of you have been talking of it and even looking forward to it. Have nothing to do with it. Listen; it's like this. Have you ever been out for a late autumn walk in the closing part of the afternoon, and suddenly looked up to realize that the leaves have practically all gone? You hadn't realized it. And you notice that the sun has set already, the day gone before you knew it—and with that a cold wind blows across the landscape. That's retirement.

As History Grows Dim

AS HISTORY GROWS DIM

(All that will be left of our Forgotten Worthies in a future dictionary)

GLADSTONE—a bag, travelling-bag with a specially wide mouth.

VICTORIA—low carriage, with a broad seat.

PRINCE ALBERT—a stuffed coat, very long, formal and never unbuttoned.

BISMARCK—a specially fat German rump steak, not popular now.

SALISBURY—another steak, English, made of what was left over from a Bismarck.

CHATEAUBRIAND—a French beefsteak, made of something else.

GOETHE (pronounced goat-ee)—a form of chinbeard once worn in Arkansas.

LINCOLN—a kind of car, formerly very popular.

WELLINGTON—a long boot, high sole.

BLUCHER—short boot with a low sole.

CARDINAL WOLSEY—a brand of gents' underwear.

HENRY CLAY—a cigar.

JEFFERSON—a hotel, avenue, or post-office.

NAPOLEON, WASHINGTON, CAESAR, SAMSON—trade names used in the plumbing business for bath-room fixtures.

MARIE ANTOINETTE, JOSEPHINE, MARIE LOUISE,

EUGENIE—trade names used in ladies' under-wear.

KING EDWARD, BONNIE PRINCE CHARLIE, CLAVER-HOUSE, ROBERT BRUCE—stallions with a pedi-gree.

MATTHEW, MARK, LUKE & JOHN—side streets in Montreal.

Twenty Cents' Worth of Murder

TWENTY CENTS' WORTH OF MURDER

I AM one of those who like each night, after the fret and worry of the day, to enjoy about twenty cents' worth of murder before turning off the light and going to sleep. Twenty cents a night is about the cost of this, for first-class murder by our best writers. Ten-cent murder is apt to be either stale or too suggestive of crime. But I am sure that I am only one of uncounted thousands of crime readers who feel that the health and enjoyment gained is well worth the price, and share my gratitude toward the brilliant galaxy of crime writers who supply our needs. I could name them if I wished to, but everyone knows them so well that it is needless.

They will not therefore take it amiss if I offer them a few suggestions, endorsed I am sure by the same thousands of readers, still uncounted, as to what we want and what we don't want in our current reading.

In the first place—if you don't mind—don't kill the victim too soon. We like to get to know him a little first. I mean, don't start with his *body*. Don't have Inspector Higginbottom summoned hastily in paragraph 2 of page 1 to the Mansions Apartments because there's a dead body just found upstairs. The thrill is too short. We lost interest. Even when it turns out that there's been "foul play" it doesn't rouse us; we expected it. Nor even when it turns out that the dead

183

man is a leading member of the Stock Exchange; that'
all right, we never heard of him anyway.

Oh, no, give us a chance to learn to know the man
a little, and like him, and then his death is like tha
of a friend; or let him be such a mean hound that we
get to hate him; then when his body is found, who i
happier than we are?

Now another little point. When you do find his body
don't have a string of people, a houseful of them, who
have to be under suspicion one after the other, so
that we can see it all coming—the butler, the private
secretary, the French maid, the handy man (too handy
perhaps)—well, everybody knows the standing list. All
these people commit murders. To these are added the
guests; after all, do we really know them? And, now
we think of it, even the family lawyer there over night
—family lawyers are often crooked. So every one o
these has to be "eliminated," one after another. All
right for the author at ten cents a word for elimina
tion, but poor stuff for us, even at a cent a page.

And, oh, yes, with this, please cut out the diagram
that goes with it, called *Plan of Arundel House*
Ground Floor, Upper Floor. It's a bum drawing, any
way, done by the author, of course, to make it look
circumstantial. But it's the same plan, as a matter o
fact, that I've seen for twenty-one years—Arunde
House, or Wisteria Lodge, or No. I Jefferson Avenue
It's all cut into little rooms with gaps for door
marked "study," "bedroom," "bath"—one bath for al
those people—and in one room is a little diagram lik
a sausage marked "body." Well, I can't study all tha

out; I have no time. Never mind explaining what window "gives" on the lawn and what other windows "give" on what; windows always "give" in detective stories. In real life they are made to go up and down. And the French windows on the ground floor of Arundel House (Plan I), never mind explaining which side they're bolted on; I can't follow it.

Oh, yes, and fingerprints. Don't have any. Really we're all tired of them. As a matter of fact I'm glad to notice that a good many of the best people are cutting them out. Inspector Higginbottom shakes his head and murmurs "gloves." It seems that practically all people who are thinking of murder go round in gloves. I've noticed them on the street.

The same with footprints—though I am not so sure about them. The old footprints that Sherlock used to trace are, of course, clean out of date. But the new scheme of Sherlock's scientific successor—you all know who it is I mean—the new scheme of blowing powder into a footprint of mud, filling it up with cement and then taking out a perfect overshoe; that's still good stuff.

Now as to your detective himself—but no, I almost despair of trying to give advice. All I can say, and I speak for all of us, is mostly negative. Don't, of course, make him long and thin; that's dead; but, for Heaven's sake, not fat. Don't have him go without sleep, or go without food, often for three or four hours at a stretch. Keep him decently fed, and, for our sake, not for his, give him drinks, plenty and often. Do you remember how, under prohibition, all the sleuth hounds had to begin to drink tea? You remember how the great detective would sit and think things out, "stirring his tea"! I don't believe you can do it. Take some whisky and, my! you'll begin to think fast.

There's one standard English crime writer, to whom I can never be sufficiently grateful, who makes a point, at every emergency in his story, of giving his characters a "stiff whisky and soda." Inspector Higginbottom, as soon as he realizes that the body is that of Sir Charles, goes to the sideboard and pours out a "stiff whisky and soda" all round! That's the stuff! I can read that all night. . . . And the criminals themselves get it even better. The moment they feel themselves in a corner—what's that word we use? Oh, yes, "trapped"—they pour out a drink, a whole tumblerful of neat brandy. Then they don't feel "trapped" at all. You can't trap a man full of that.

Of course you would ask why just whisky and not champagne? It's too expensive. There is, as everybody knows, one prince of mystery story tellers who never conducts a crime without giving us at least half an hour at Monte Carlo, with "frosted champagne cocktails" and a Rumanian princess to look at! But it feels extravagant, for anybody brought up in a plain home with just whisky.

And yet such is the contrariety of things here in this author—I mean the one with the whisky and soda (all my associated readers know exactly who it is I mean) so fine about the drinks and yet falling into another fault that always exasperates us—I mean filling his books with descriptions and scenery. He begins

practically always, with a "market town"—Hellborough, or some such place, where they talk broad something. We can stand for a street or two, but when it
comes to the town hall, dating from Edward the Con-
fessor, we pass. Scenery we don't need at all, except
to take it fast, like a tourist in a picture gallery. You
see, those of us who have read crime stories for
twenty or thirty years have got in our minds a collection of scenes like what they call the "sets" in a ten-
twenty-thirty theatre. "Market town of Hellborough"
—correct, we have it; "purlieus of Chicago"—right,
here you are; "drawing-room of the rectory"—that's
it—or not, not that, that's a "bar-room in Denver."
But anyway we've got all our "sets" and a collection
of weather; it's odd the junk we carry in our minds
as an equipment for reading. However, that's another
topic.

.   .   .   .

And there's this. As you get nearer the end of the
story, don't have them all chase one another round.
I mean all the characters, bandits, detectives, etc., in
a sort of grand climax. You know the kind of thing
I mean—in and out of cellars, down rat holes, out
through outhouses. Poor old Edgar Wallace—there,
I hadn't meant to mention names, but never mind—
could never get away from this: the sleuth trapped by
the bandit, thrown into a cellar, water turned on,
reaches his throat, dives out through a sewer, runs
round in front, nails up the door, bandit trapped, goes
to the attic, detective follows, detective trapped, bandit on roof, leaps into an aeroplane, detective crawls

through a fly-screen, leaps into another aeroplane—
zoop! They're both gone. We have to begin over
again.

And here's a point of importance for the conclusion itself. Don't be afraid to hang the criminal at
the end. Better lay the story, if you can, in a jurisdic-
tion where they hang them, because, to us readers, the
electric chair sounds too uncomfortable. But hanging
is old and respectable, and if you like you can use such
a phrase as "went to the scaffold" or "went to the gal-
lows." That's as simple as Old Mother Hubbard. But
I mean we want him *hanged;* don't let him fall into the
sea out of his aeroplane. It's not good enough. Hold
him tight by the pants, till you get him to the gal-
lows. And *don't* let your criminal get ill in prison,
or get so badly wounded or so heavily poisoned that
he never gets tried because he is "summoned to a
higher court." Honestly, you can't *get* a higher criminal court than the State Court of Appeal. There isn't
one.

I'll stop there. Other readers may have suggestions.

Reader's Junk

READER'S JUNK

In writing about detective stories as above, I stated that, for me, it wasn't necessary for the writer of such a story to put into his book a plan of the house that was the scene of the murder. I said that I carried in my head, from much reading of crime, a plan of the house already made, cut up into bedrooms, with a passage-way, and one "bath" (for everybody) and a shape like a sausage lying loose in one room and marked "body." Sometimes the house was called "Wisteria Lodge" and sometimes "Arundel House" or No. 1 Jefferson Avenue. It would do for any of them.

I had no sooner written this than I realized that it was only one sample of the quantity of junk which any reader carries round in his mind, ready to use, like the "sets" of a repertory theatre. In fact everybody has picked up a whole lumber room of them—country houses (for murder); shooting-lodges (for mystery); castles, for use in the Middle Ages; and a collection of city sets, such as a "midnight restaurant," an "Alhambra Grill," an "obscure tobacconist's," a "den of vice," a "purlieus" (or do you have to have two of them?), the "left side" of Paris, the West side of Chicago. Everybody knows them and keeps a collection of them. Most of them no doubt are a long way off reality.

A shooting-lodge, for instance—I've never seen one.

What do you shoot in it? And why lodge? I always
picture it made of cedar in the rough, set up end on,
with a lot of gable corners. My shooting-lodge is really
a compound made of a half-and-half mixture of Old
Vienna and a Canadian lumber shanty. A den of vice!
For that I use a lot of smoke, a guttering candle, with
plenty of grease; that makes it "murky." Or dear old
Monte Carlo—I've never seen the place, but I have
it there all ready for use like slipping in a lantern slide.
There's the Casino, come in. I built it when I was
about ten years old and had never seen one; I can't
ever get it straight; it's too much like a barn. They
are playing "baccarat" in it, but I am afraid the baccarat table is too much like a barn supper (I was
brought up in the country). All around Monte Carlo
are a set of huge flowers that I keep—taken as names
years ago and never seen—such as hibiscus and climb-
ing rancenculus and flowering funeraria. No doubt you
have a lot of them too. The effect is vague but gor-
geous. The flowers and shrubs are used to bury the
bungalows, because from my earliest recollection
bungalows are always "buried in flowers." My bungalows are a bum lot; they were copied originally from
summer cottages on Lake Simcoe, and it's hard to get
them plastered and put "plinths" on them and cor-
nices. No, they're all wrong. I admit it.

But the point that I am groping toward is the inquiry as to the effect on literature, I mean on the appreciation of it, of this accumulation in the reader's
mind of a set of preconceptions, pictures and ready-
made characters. It seems to me that it must act on

the mind as hardening of the arteries does in the body. Presently nothing can get through. What's the good of trying to tell a desert island story to a reader like you or me, who has owned a desert island for fifty years, yellow sand, a rivulet of pure water (that was a piece of luck) and a banyan tree, a form of bread and of which the "fibres" can be used to make fish lines.

It's the same with the characters. We all have a stock of them ready for use like marionettes in a child's theatre. For example a "benevolent old gentleman"—what a peach he seemed when we first read of him at twelve; what a nut now. You see no new benevolent old gentleman can get a chance with us; the minute the author names him we say "Right oh!" and substitute our own. Personally I always, in reading fiction, use my own benevolent old gentleman, my own family lawyer, my own curate, my own ship's bosun and all the rest of them. I take them to each new book as people take their own food to a basket picnic.

.   .   .   .

If someone of a critical turn were to follow up this train of thought perhaps it might prove interesting— help to explain why interest flags in age, and why authors rise and fall. This much is certain. Whenever we can get away from preconceptions and stock pictures and take our fiction straight, as children do, it stands out with marvellous clarity and interest. I find an instance of this in the great vogue that the "Western Picture" enjoys all over the world. You will see an English audience (right out of the purlieus, or of the bungalows) sit enthralled as they watch the sheriff's posse chase through the sage brush, see the desperado shoot up the saloon, and the real train fall through the actual trestle bridge.

The reason is that it's all new, or still new enough. It hasn't—not yet, or only partly—been all raked over like a dust heap and used again and again. That's why, for the present, even for English audiences, it beats things out of English history ten ways. Don't show me Queen Elizabeth getting into her barge off the stone steps beside the Thames. Bless me, I've seen the woman, and the same steps, since I was eight. And the courtiers, in the queer little puffed pants, why, I keep a set of them given me by Alexander Dumas in the middle eighties. . . . But the sheriff's daughter, shooting Lobscouse, the Indian brave, with her father's derringer (18 inches long)!—ah! There's a girl for you!

Of course it can't last. Already the new generation are gathering up their sets of scenery and their characters on strings. The Sheriff of Cheyenne, Wyoming, will soon be as dead flat as Henry of Navarre, and Lobscouse the Indian will fall back into second class with Queen Victoria, and Mollie of the Ranges (who shot him) will just look like Charlotte Corday or Marie Antoinette.

And then, of course, something else will turn up, to catch again the colours of the morning. If it didn't, our literature would fall asleep, like the dead classics of China; would turn into "sacred books," read in the dust of pyramids. But that time is not yet. As a civilization we are still only just past sunrise.

LITTLE STORIES FOR GOOD LUCK

THREE ON EACH

When I was teaching at Upper Canada College fifty years ago, we took corporal punishment for granted. I myself had been "licked" at school and as a master I "licked" the boys without any compunction or after-thought about it. As a matter of fact corporal punishment, which is after all the same thing as physical torture, can only exist on those terms—that nobody thinks about it.

But even in those days there were some people who found the idea revolting and couldn't bear to think of it. One of my college friends felt like this. So I said to him one day, "Fred, if you'll come down to Upper Canada College this afternoon at three o'clock when school ends, I'll be certain to have two or three boys who have to take a caning and you'll see how simple and normal it is."

But that day something seemed wrong in class. Not a boy "did" anything all day—just quiet ordinary behaviour and lessons all first rate.

It looked at three o'clock as if I would have no one to "lick." But I didn't want to disappoint my friend. So I said to the "worst" boy in the class, one of those fine young toughs who are really the *best:*

"Urquhart, you'll stay in after three when the class goes."

"Please, sir," he protested, "what's that for?"

"That'll be all, Urquhart," I answered, "don't be impertinent."

At that moment my friend arrived and I said to him very gravely: "I'm afraid I have a delinquent boy to deal with here before I can go. But if you'll just sit down I won't be a minute."

"Please, sir," clamoured Urquhart as I got out the cane, "what's this for?"

"Urquhart," I said, "please don't make things worse by lying about it. You're to have three on each, or I must report you to the principal for refusing to take a caning."

That was enough for a decent boy like Urquhart. To refuse to take a caning and go and blab to the principal was pretty low business for a boy of his spirit.

He stood up and took his three on each, like the little man he was.

I would have felt pretty mean about it if it hadn't been that after he had had his licking Urquhart said:

"I want to apologize, sir, for trying to lie out of it. Only I didn't see how you knew about it."

But I never knew what Urquhart had done: except that, as all schoolmasters know, a high-spirited boy has always done *something*.

NOTHING MISSING

I was saying the other day how absent-minded professors are and how simple-minded—I mean in the good sense of the term. They have no notion of the narrow exactness of business.

A case in point is that of my friend Cartwright Trope who was a lecturer in the University of Chicago at a time when I was a graduate student there, many years ago.

Trope and his wife were going away for the summer and were moving their furniture out of their flat into storage. Trope came to me and asked me if I would do him a favour and I said, certainly.

"We're going away by this evening's train," he said, "but the furniture men don't come till tomorrow after-noon. I was wondering if you would mind"—here he produced a long paper with a list of things written on it—"it's really a lot to ask—but would you, perhaps, go over to the flat and just sit around while they move the things out—it's only two loads—and just check them off on this list and then you could post the list to me, and I'll know it's all right."

I said it was a mere nothing, and that I'd do it gladly and Trope went away much relieved.

Next day I didn't bother to go near his flat. I just took a blue pencil and made a little mark against each item on the list, some slanting one way and some an-other, and some a little light and some a little heavy. Then I posted the paper to Trope.

A month later in Toronto we met at an afternoon tea and Trope told of how kind I'd been. "Every item!" he said, "every item, and there must have been a hundred—and every single one checked off!"

I've often wondered since what happened.

THINKING OF TOMORROW

I WAS grieved to see by the papers a few weeks ago that the world has lost that kindly Irish poet, W. B. Yeats. I knew him a little bit, years ago. Unlike most literary celebrities, he looked the part. His face would assume at times a look of far-away abstraction, such as only a poet would wear.

One time when "Billy" Yeats was in Montreal lecturing, I gave a supper party for him at the University Club—a large round table filled with admiring women, and silent husbands. There came a lull in the conversation during which Yeats' face assumed the far-away look of which I speak. The ladies gazed at him in rapt admiration. At last one said:

"What are you thinking about, Mr. Yeats?"

"Thinking of tomorrow," he answered in his rich musical voice, "and wondering!"

You could feel the ripple of sympathetic interest among the ladies: the word "tomorrow" carries such infinite meaning.

"Wondering what?" someone ventured in a half whisper.

"Wondering," said Yeats, "if there is breakfast on the Boston train."

.   .   .   .

After all, poets have to feed.

INFORMATION WHILE YOU DRINK

AMONG the figures of the vanished past whom I regret, is the old-time bartender—I mean, the bartender at his best.

There he stood behind his bar, mopping up the foam, urbane, polite, neat in his wicker sleeves and with his hair flattened with oil—courteous, obliging, tireless.

He never drank.

"Have one on me, Billy?"

"Thanks, I'll take a cigar."

But his especial forte was information—the latest horse race, the coming ball game, the time of all the "shows" and the "records" of the sprinters and scullers —in short, all any "sport" could need.

Beyond that he handed out general information, and beyond that conversation to order as desired.

Vilhjalmur Stefansson informs us somewhere that Eskimos always tell you what they think you want to hear; they answer a question according to what they think you'd like.

Well, the bartenders were like that.

"Fine day! Billy."

"It sure is."

"Looks like rain, eh, Billy?"

"It certainly does."

But I am thinking here of a specially illustrative case of bartenders' information that happened within my own experience. It was in Montreal away back in

1902 or 1901—at any rate in the year, whichever it was, when Émile Zola died.

I had gone into the bar of the old Prince of Wales Hotel to get a drink before dinner, and stood reading the evening paper while I drank it.

My eye suddenly caught a news item and I looked up—forgetting in my surprise just who I was talking to—and said to the bartender:

"Billy, you don't mean to tell me that Émile Zola's dead?"

Billy shook his head sadly and went on wiping the bar with his cloth as he said:

"I think he must be. I ain't seen him round anyway for a week or more."

NO PLACE FOR GENTLEMEN

EVERYBODY knows how hard it is in English to use the word "gentleman" in any fixed meaning. I have heard it defined by a Sunday School boy as meaning "a man with a gold watch who loves Jesus." But the test seems a little too exacting. On the other hand, I remember a bygone citizen of my home town, an industrious man with a large family, who used to say, "My motto is, no *gentleman* in this family."

But the most definite beam of light I ever got on it reached me forty years ago when I lived in Chicago as a student, and had the honor of meeting a friend of my brother Jim, a Mr. Donnegan, who had just finished three months in one of the state prisons in Illinois, for failing to grasp the idea of the new pure food law.

Jim and I went into a bar to get a beer and Mr. Donnegan was standing in the centre of a group of admirers.

He beckoned to Jim and we joined them and Jim said proudly, "Stephen, meet Mr. Donnegan. He's just come back from three months in Joliet."

Mr. Donnegan shook hands, but he said: "Not in Joliet, though, Jimmy. No thank you; I was in Elgin."

"All right," Jim said, "but I don't see that it makes much difference."

"All the difference in the world, Jimmy," said Mr. Donnegan. "I don't want to knock any place or any crowd; but I'll just tell you the fellows in Elgin, Jimmy, are a set of gentlemen. I won't say that for Joliet."

The lapse of forty years has prevented me from being sure as to which is this. But the warning stands that one of these two is no place for a gentleman.

"WE HAVE WITH US TONIGHT"

PUBLIC speaking is more or less of an ordeal even for those who have to undertake it constantly. Worse than all is speaking at a dinner, because you have to wait your turn and feel it coming for hours. Next time you are at a public dinner notice the men at the head table who sit and eat celery by the bunch and never stop. Those are the men who are going to speak.

I don't say that trained speakers are nervous. No. They wish the chairman would announce that the rest of the meeting is cancelled because of smallpox, or that the hotel would catch fire, or that there would be an earthquake. But they're not nervous.

But if speaking is an ordeal to *them,* what it is to those who have never spoken. Some men go through life and never have to speak; they rise to wealth and standing with the fear of it in the background—fear, with an element of temptation.

Such a one was my senior acquaintance of long ago, Mr. Gritterly—no harm to name him—general manager of one of the Toronto banks. He had just retired, without ever speaking in public, when a Bankers' Three Days Convention came to town and they invited Mr. Gritterly to speak at the dinner.

He accepted, hung in the wind, flew round the flame —and finally, on the opening day, sent a note that he was called out of town for the evening.

I saw him round the hotel next morning. He was telling me how sorry he was to have missed the opportunity. He told me a lot of things he could have said about branch banking. He said, too, that he would like to have had a sly joke, very good-natured of course, about the American Treasury system. It was too bad, he said, he'd been called out of town. He had even intended, just in an offhand way, to get off one or two quotations from Shakespeare (he had them in his pocket). One read—"I know a bank whereon a wild thyme grows—" Gritterly thought that would get a laugh, eh? Too bad, he said, that he couldn't get that off.

"But, Mr. Gritterly," I said, "you're making a mistake. They didn't have the dinner last night. The

trains were so late they only had the inaugural address. The dinner's tonight. You'll probably get an invitation—"

And as I spoke a boy brought it to him on a tray.

"So you see you'll be able to tell them about branch
banking."

"Yes," said Mr. Gritterly, "yes."

"And the jokes about the U. S. Treasury."

"Yes," said Mr. Gritterly, "quite so."

All day Gritterly was round the hotel pulling the
little bits of Shakespeare out of his pocket.

But the thing beat him.

In due course at the dinner the chairman announced:
"I regret very much that Mr. Gritterly will not be
able to speak. His speech, of which he gave me an
outline, would have been a great treat. Unfortunately
he had to leave tonight"—the chairman consulted his
notes—"for Japan. With your permission I will take
on myself to cable our representatives and I am sure
they'll be glad to get up a dinner for Mr. Gritterly at
Tokio."

Gritterly got the invitation on board ship and went
right on to Hong Kong. The bankers there received a
cable and organized a lunch. Gritterly had gone on to
Singapore but the bankers followed him up, and he
left for Calcutta. They lost him somewhere in Thibet.
He may have entered the monastery there. For many
people that would be preferable to speaking.

A HUMBLE LOVER

HAVE you ever noticed how much attracted we all are by humility? From vainglorious people, conscious of talent, of power, we turn aside. Let them have success if they will. It's theirs for the asking. But appeal they cannot have; that is for the meek, for the failures, for the people who might have been but never were.

This is especially true of love. The humble lover, aware of his own nothingness, goes to our hearts. The pathos of unrequited love, devotion without return, is among the oldest of human stories.

One such humble lover I knew and here chronicle. I set him down as he was. Judge him for yourself.

He had reached the age when he felt that it was time to get married. Other fellers did. Joe—that was his name—was close to thirty.

He said to me one night, "I think I'd like to get married." Then he said nothing for quite a time and presently: "There's a girl on the next street—"

That was as far as he could get for a while, but no doubt it meant a lot. It has, to many of us—"a girl on the next street."

So I asked:

"Do you know her, Joe?"

"Mother does," he answered. "She belongs to mother's morning musical club and mother often invites some of the girls to play music at the house."

"And you haven't met her?"

"Yes, I have in a way. The other afternoon she left her guitar here by accident and mother asked me to take it home to her; so I took it round to her house and a maid came to the door and I said 'This is Miss Carson's guitar,' and she said 'Thank you. Do you want to see Miss Carson?' and I said 'No.' "

"And that's all you've seen of her?"

"No," Joe said, "the other day when she came to the house I was just outside and she said to me: 'How do you do? It's a lovely day, isn't it?' And I said, 'It sure is!'—just like that—'It sure is.' And she went in and I went on out."

From then on my friend gave me details of his humble courtship.

Miss Carson, it seems, left her rubbers at the house and Joe fetched them home and gave them to her father. Her father said, "It's a nice night, isn't it?" So that would seem to mean that he looked on things pretty favourably, eh?

I asked Joe, a little later in his courtship, if he had spoken yet to Miss Carson about marriage. He said no, but he had discussed it with his mother. His mother was all for it. He was going to wait awhile and then talk to his father. If his father was for it and his mother and if I was for it, that made three. He told me that the other morning he had ridden down town in the same street car as Miss Carson and she said, "Isn't it a lovely morning?" and he said, 'It sure is"—just as easy as that. Too bad, he had to get off the next street after she got on.

Soon after that Joe read me a letter of proposal

that he had prepared. It began: "It is no longer pos
sible for me to restrain the expression of the senti
ments with which our intercourse has inspired me—'
"Fine, isn't it," he said. "I got it out of a book. I'l
start it again. It's good. . . ."

I was not surprised when Joe sent me word a day o
two later that he wanted to see me.

"Did you get an answer from Miss Carson?" I
asked him.

"Fine!" he said. "A dandy letter. Everything's O.K
It seems that she isn't thinking of getting married, so
it's all right; and she thanked me for writing to her
and said my letter was swell."

My heart began to sink with sympathy.

"Too bad, Joe," I said.

"I'm not so sure," he answered. "I find there's an
other girl on the same street, two houses nearer, tha
perhaps I can get. I've talked with mother about it
she's all for it."

.   .   .   .

After Joe's case, I have never felt quite so sure
about the humble and the meek. Perhaps they're jus
slow, eh?—

THE MAGIC OF FINANCE

I HAVE an artist friend who is the best portrait painter
in Canada. This will at once identify him to himself
But as it will also identify about a dozen others to
themselves, I will simply call him Jares and let it go
at that.

Jares told me this story about the beginning of his making his fortune.

The time came in his upward rise when he got several hundred dollars for each portrait, then passed into the thousands and presently he got his first *real* order—a commission to paint the portrait of a New York millionaire stock-broker for five thousand dollars.

The "sittings" in New York went along very pleasantly and satisfactorily. The millionaire stock-broker evidently took a fancy to the rising young genius.

When the last sitting came he said to the artist:

"Mr. Jares, I must see about having your cheque made out. But, tell me first, what are you going to do now for the next two or three months?"

Jares said that he was going to take a holiday in Brittany.

"Good," said the broker. "I have a proposal to make. Suppose you leave this money with us and see what we can do with it while you're away. Mind," he added as a caution, "I don't say we're wizards you know; people get exaggerated ideas. But suppose you just leave it and see?"

Jares assented with delight.

He went away to Brittany, had a three months' holiday and returned to New York.

He went round to the broker's office and sent in his card. The millionaire, after a moment's hesitation, received him most cordially.

"Mr. Jares!" he said. "Why, yes, of course! You left five thousand in an open account with us—of course, of course!"

He pushed a bell button and gave a few words of instructions to a lady secretary. "Just ask them," he said, "to send a memorandum."

In a few minutes the lady secretary returned and gave a paper to the broker with a few words in low voice.

"Well, well," said the millionaire, "is that so! Mr. Jares, this is very interesting. We lost that five thousand—it seems. That's the way things go, you know. It's lost—very interesting. Well, well—I mustn't keep you. Drop in some time when you're in New York again."

Jares left—he had seen what they could do with it.

HE GUESSED RIGHT

THERE is a certain line of anecdote which often goes under the name of "grim humour." This means humour that turns on actual injury or death. Personally I've always felt doubtful about it.

To explain what is meant, here is a story, actually true, of a happening in Toronto at the old Rossin House, long ago. The baggage man who was putting trunks into the elevator (from the service chute) was called away from his job and didn't realize in the poor light that the elevator had gone up a couple of stories and was above him. He swung the door open, called in a cheery voice, "All right, Bill, down she does," jumped in—and broke his leg two stories below.

In this kind of "grim humour," as I say, I find little

attraction. Yet the Scotch seem to like it—they love
the familiar stories of Scotchmen at their wives' fu-
nerals, or the story of the Scotch judge who sentenced
to death a man he used to play chess with, and said—
"And that's checkmate for you, Andrew."

But one such story I can quote from memory, not
actually of my own but of my brother George. It con-
cerns the death of a man in the power-house of a western Ontario town (I'll name it no closer than that)
where George was working, installing electrical equipment. In those days electricity was new and conse-
quently dangerous.

One morning the assistant man of the power-house
came running to the workers on the line to say that his
boss had been killed.

They went down with the chief of police to the
power-house and there was the unhappy man, dead,
laid out flat on the cement floor, his arms extended.

They looked at him in horror.

"How do you suppose it happened, Joe?" asked
the chief of police.

"Why, I can't see how it could," said the assistant—
"the only possible way it seems to me is that he may
have picked up this terminal with one hand"—as he
said it, Joe picked up the terminal—"and then put his
other out in contact with—"

Bing! And the second man was laid out beside the
first. Joe had guessed right.

  . . . .

Now as a matter of fact I am glad to record that
the second man, though knocked unconscious, was not

really killed.

But when my brother George, who is a real story teller, tells this story, he not only kills the second man but the chief of police—who undertook to explain it to the mayor of the town, and then the mayor and half of the town council.

Nothing like Art for Art's sake.

ELECTRIC SERVICE

I was talking the other day about "grim humour," and told the story of the man who was killed in the Ontario power-house.

I afterwards remembered another example of grim humour that is recalled from the days when I used to go on lecture trips in the United States.

I was to lecture in an Ohio city and a local lawyer kindly met me at the train and drove me to my hotel. On the way he indicated points of interest.

"That's our jail," he said, stopping the car for a minute beside a grim building that walled one side of the street and he added, "I had a queer experience with a man in there a month or two back."

"What was that?" I asked.

"Well," he said, "this feller was in there under sentence of electrocution, and our firm got a letter from a law firm in Chicago which read:

" 'We understand that Mr. Joseph Smith is a client of yours, in which case please inform him that if he does not pay the account for $18.50 on which we have been suing him, we must proceed to more drasti neasures.'

"We wrote back in answer," continued the lawyer—
' 'You are correct in supposing that Mr. Joseph Smith
s a client of ours. He is at present in the jail here
awaiting electrocution, but if you can think of any-
hing more drastic, please proceed to it right away.' ''

.   .   .   .

The lawyer, having told his story, proceeded, after
he American fashion, to hang another piece onto it.

"Yes, sir," he continued, "that feller was up in that
corner cell, and I went to see him—when we knew
ae'd no chance—and asked him if there was anything
we could do for him."

" 'Yes,' says he, 'there is; I don't exactly like that
electric sign I see across the street every time I go to
he window.' ''

The lawyer stopped speaking and began to start his
car.

"And what was the sign?" I asked.

"It's still there," he said. "You can read it."

He pointed, and I looked up and saw a sign that
read, *Something in Electricity for Everybody*.

OUR VANISHED INDUSTRIES

MOST of us, I think, admit that in their way the Mari-
ime Provinces are the finest part of Canada. I don't
mean by reason of their resources, but on account of
he inhabitants themselves. You get there that fine,
sturdy type of people from the British Isles—a type
hat was rather than is—honorable, courageous, con-

tent with little, and valuing intellectual and moral life rather than material. Indeed the making of men and the "export of brains" has always seemed a leading industry of the Maritimes.

I had a very special opportunity to learn this when I was invited there for a week's lecture tour after I had been appointed to my chair at McGill. I not only had occasion to appreciate the type of men bred in that environment, but to form some idea of the process and method of making them.

At my first lecture I was the guest of a bank manager in Moncton, and at the close of the evening we sat together over a pipe in his comfortable study, and we fell to talking of his earlier days.

". . . And how did you get your bank training?" I asked him.

"I learned it," he answered, "as a boy on a Nova Scotia schooner of the old days. Every time I was told to do anything I had to do it right off and without any question or I got a swift kick in the backside. That's the training that fitted me later for a bank."

The next day when I had moved on to another town, I was talking with the mayor of the town about his life and career. "Yes," he said, "I'm a self-made man and I'm not ashamed of it: or rather I won't say I'm a self-made man—I'll say that the beginning of my success was made for me as a boy working on a Nova Scotia schooner."

"How was that?" I asked.

"Well," said the mayor, "if I was told to do something I had to hop to it and do it or I got a swift kick in the backside."

As I went on through the Maritime Provinces I began to realize that this early start in life had been shared by most of the leading men. One of the judges had, according to his own statement, got his first grasp on the principles of law by getting a swift kick in the backside. The same treatment had started men in medicine, education, and public life, and for business it was universal.

I struck only one doubtful case. I had met a most cultivated man, well up in years, a professor of divinity in a church university. He talked to me modestly of his early struggles.

"Life was for me," he said, "a very arduous path. I doubt if I could have walked it if I had not had—I hope you won't think my reasoning absurd—"

"I know," I interrupted, "you had a swift kick in the backside on a Nova Scotia schooner."

The old man looked at me calmly.

"No," he said quietly, "I was going to say, a belief in the efficacy of prayer . . ."

I felt that I had got in wrong and was humiliated. But it was all right. The old man was silent for a moment and then he said:

"The other may have helped, too."

You see they can't tell a lie in the Maritimes even if they try to.

So I've been thinking about this treatment; perhaps there's something in it. So many of our public men are accused of inefficiency and indifference. Couldn't we try the idea—eh?

COULDN'T SLEEP A WINK

I OFTEN think that all this "insomnia" business is about ninety per cent nonsense; I mean—the people who come down in the morning and tell you they "couldn't sleep a wink," "never closed an eye," and all that. They may think so but as a matter of fact they probably had their eyes closed up for hours at a stretch.

Years ago when I was a young man in a boarding house in Toronto, my brother George came down to stay the night. There was no spare room in the boarding-house, and, what was worse, only one bed—although it was a double one—in mine. But the trouble was that we both hated "sleeping double" and knew that there was mighty little chance of getting a decent night's rest that way.

However, we took it in good part, went to bed and decided just to lie there, sleepless, and let it go at that.

In the morning, after it got to be real daylight, I spoke and said to George, "Did you get much sleep?" "Not a damn minute," he said. "Neither could I," I answered, "so I just lay here; I could hear every sound all night." "So could I," George said.

Then we put our heads up from the bed-clothes and noticed for the first time that the bed was covered about two inches deep with plaster. The ceiling had fallen on us in the night.

But we hadn't noticed it. We had "insomnia."

GO TO MOTHER

MANY years ago, when I was teaching at Upper Canada College and was still young enough to go to the races and that sort of thing, I struck a holiday and started off for the Woodbine Races.

When I got to the place just north of Toronto where the cars branched in different ways, whom should I meet but my old friend Canon Drone, waiting for a car.

He stopped me with a pleasant inquiry of where I was heading for.

"Why, Canon Drone," I said, "I was just going to make up my mind whether I'd go out to the Woodbine Races or take the Radial Railway and go up to Sutton and spend the day with mother."

I hadn't had the least intention of going up to see mother. But it sounded a good thing to work off on a clergyman—like handing him something.

But the old Canon took it up too seriously.

"Stephen," he said, lifting his hand in the air and speaking in his best pulpit voice, "Go-to-*mother!*"

You know what a quiver a really good clergyman can put into the word "mother!"

"Resist temptation," said the Canon; "get on that car—that's the one—and go to mother."

He had me beaten. I saw no way round it. He wasn't going to move, so I ended by getting on the car and going up to Sutton to spend the day with mother. That is—I spent it in painting the garden fence.

Mother never wasted a visitor.

That evening when I got back to the city I met a friend of mine at the car junction.

"You weren't at the races?" he said.

"No, I spent the day up at Sutton with mother."

"Too bad," he said; "you missed a big day. By the way, I saw your old friend Canon Drone out there having a whale of a time. He's a great old sport. He told me he'd made twenty dollars."

FIVE DOLLARS, RIGHT NOW

SOME time ago, quite a few years back, we had an "old home week" in my town of Orillia. Among those who came back was Eddie Foote who had been away at Napanee, or somewhere, for about twenty years.

Like all people who come back for home week, he was just brim-full of interest in all old acquaintances.

He stopped me on the street and shook hands enthusiastically, and began asking about my brothers and where they all were. I happen to have a lot of brothers —we were six at the start—and, like all large families, we scattered all over. Some of my brothers went west and some to the States; I was the only one who didn't go far.

So Eddie began, "Where's your brother Charlie, now?"

I said, "Oh, Charlie went out to B. C. about four years ago and—"

"Is that so?" Eddie cut in. "Good old Charlie. Say! I'd give five dollars to see Charlie right now. And where's Teddy?"

"Teddy lives in Calgary."

"You don't say! Good old Ted! I'd give five dollars to see Teddy right now."

I realized that Eddie Foote had only one formula for the language of delight; for all earthly joys of re-union he'd pay five dollars right now. He went right on and put another five dollars on my brother Jim in Chicago. Then he said:

"And where's your brother George? I'd give five dollars right now to see old George again."

"This is George," I answered, "coming up the street; and that's Jim with Teddy coming up behind him. That's fifteen dollars for the three, Eddie, and Charlie's coming in on the afternoon train; that'll be twenty. They're all back for the home week."

Eddie didn't pay up. He laughed it off; but he took the story back with him to Napanee, or wherever it is, and tells it as one on himself. I understand that he adds that he'd give five dollars to see Steve right now! He'd better watch out.

ARE PROFESSORS ABSENT-MINDED?

YEARS ago when I lived on the Côte des Neiges Road, in Montreal, I used often to have a little group of my fellow professors up to dinner. Sometimes their con-versation in the study upstairs after dinner was really good.

I recall one evening when we fell to discussing the old question, are professors really absent-minded. All

the men present, alert, intelligent men of today, utterly
ridiculed the idea. They admitted that the professors
of a generation back—the old fellows under whom
they had studied—were ludicrously absent-minded, but
claimed that the professor of today is another kind of
man. One of them told an amusing story of his old
professor at Edinburgh, an old man who never, never
went out in the evening but had been persuaded to
break the rule and go to a big evening reception.

He arrived at the house about eight-thirty—the
first guest, nearly half an hour ahead of fashionable
time—and was shown up into a bedroom. He didn't
come down for so long that the hostess sent up to look
for him. He'd gone to bed and was asleep.

Another professor told of an old Oxford don who
was out for the evening and was given a bundle of
letters—about a dozen of them—to post on his way
home. He forgot them, went away to Iceland on a
geological trip for six months, then found the letters
and posted them. Inside the letters were invitations to
dinner "the day after tomorrow."

The professors laughed at the stories but said that
the idea was nonsense.

Yet next morning my telephone was kept busy for
half an hour. Two of the professors had got the
wrong overshoes, one had two walking-sticks and my
little terrier had eaten a lecture on Cicero.

LITTLE STORIES FOR GOOD LUCK   221

WANTED: A GOLD-FISH

I TOLD a story in this series about absent-minded professors. But here's a true one that I can vouch for out of my own experience at McGill.

One of our professors of physiology was out visiting one winter night, and the people at the house showed him a gold-fish that had died because the water that it was in had got frozen. The professor looked at the fish and said, "Let me take it home and I think that tomorrow I can treat it in the laboratory and revive it."

So when he started for home they wrapped the gold-fish in a bit of tissue paper and Professor Floyd put it in his overcoat pocket. It was a cold night, very late and with lots of deep snow along the street. On the way home Floyd put his hand into his coat pocket and accidently flipped out the gold-fish and it fell into the snow.

Floyd knelt down to pick it up, but he couldn't find it and stayed there on his knees groping for it. Just then a policeman came along on his beat and stopped and said, "What are you doing there?"

Professors hate to be questioned. Floyd just looked over his shoulder and said, "I am trying to find a gold-fish."

The policeman then understood that he was dealing with a mental case, and he said, coaxingly, "Now you just come along with me and I'll take you to a place where we've a whole lot of gold-fish—all you want."

"All right," Floyd said, "only just help me to get this one first."

To humour him the policeman knelt down and began groping in the snow and, first thing he knew, out came a gold-fish! He was absolutely flabbergasted.

"Great heavens!" he said. "Are there any more?"

"Maybe a whole lot," Floyd said. As the professor started off for home again, the policeman was still on his knees looking for gold-fish.

MUSHROOMS

I AM very fond of mushrooms. Often I go out from my home town to where there are some big open pastures on the third concession and gather up a whole basketful, carry them part of the way home, and then —throw them away.

Sometimes I carry them only as far as the pasture fence and throw them away there; at other times I take them part of the way home and throw them away beside the road or in a culvert. Sometimes I go alone, or sometimes with another man—someone also keen on mushrooms—and then we perhaps carry them further and don't throw them away until we are nearly back to town.

Your trouble is, you see, are the darned things mushrooms? You feel all right about it when you pick them, and then later, perhaps quite suddenly, the doubt comes—are they really mushrooms, or are they that deadly thing, what's it called, the *culex americanus?* or the *codex siniaticus?*—anyhow the kind that poisons ou in less than five minutes.

Yet it seems such a shame to throw away beautiful mushrooms, without at least trying them out, that at imes I carry my mushrooms right into town and give hem away to any friends I meet.

And that reminds me of the day I gave the mushrooms to Arthur Hart, or rather, to use the name that ie gave himself, Art 'Art. Art was a little Cockney Englishman. He was a friendly little fellow as all Cockneys are, and liked to be called by his Christian iame, Art, rather than by his surname 'Art.

As soon as he felt that he had made an acquaintance he would say, "I sy, don't call me 'Art; just call ne Art; that's good enough, ain't it?"

Then he would explain himself in more detail. "I lown't like formality. When people start, 'Art this ind 'Art that, I always sy, 'Look 'ere, ole chap, never nind that 'Art business, just call me Art.' "

Well, I was coming back one day from getting mushrooms and had just thrown my basketful into a culvert outside the town when I met my friend Webber on the street, and he gave me another basketful. I couldn't throw them away while Webber was in sight, ind I was still carrying them when I met Art.

"My 'at," he said, "those are fine mushrooms!"

I realized that there are a lot of Englishmen who know all about mushrooms. So I said, "Take them, Art, I have some at home already."

"I certainly will," Art said readily and away he vent with the mushrooms.

And the next day, first thing I knew, somebody said

to me on the street:

"Did you hear about Arthur Hart? They don't think he'll live."

"Great Caesar!" I said. "What's the matter?"—though I felt I knew.

"Poisoned, so the doctors say; something he must have eaten, only Arthur says he didn't eat anything in particular at all."

It occurred to me that if Art was going to say nothing about the mushrooms, I wouldn't mention them either, not even later on. Life has to carry these buried recollections.

However, Art got better. I saw him on the street a few days later and I said, "Art, I'm terribly sorry about giving you those mushrooms that poisoned you, and it was fine of you to say nothing about it."

"Ho, no!" Art said, "I didn't eat the mushrooms. I threw them away as soon as you were out of sight. I always do."

"But what poisoned you, Art?" I asked.

Art looked all around and put his hand to the side of his mouth and said in a low voice:

" 'Ootch!"

.   .   .   .

Funny, isn't it? We all throw away mushrooms, because a chance of one in a hundred, and take a chance (or used to in the days of which I speak) on "hootch," with the odds a hundred to one against us. There seems a sort of moral to this, but it might work the wrong way. I won't try to draw it: I'll leave the cork in it.

HELP WANTED

VERY many women can't listen. And least of all, pretty women. In a way they don't need to. They can get along without.

I am not thinking here of women who talk all the time. There are lots of those. They don't listen because they never stop talking. But I refer to the class of charming women, in society, who don't listen, especially when they are hostesses, partly because they would find it a little hard to follow, and partly because their minds are on other things.

Your delightful hostess beside you, while you tell her about your trip to Czechoslovakia, is looking you in the face with every appearance of interest. In reality she is wondering why the maid hasn't started to pass the second vegetable, or whether you know that the olives are beside you within easy reach.

No harm is done as a rule by these charming lapses of attention. Just now and again something happens.

As in the following case.

I was at a supper party in Toronto—it's a good while ago—and our young hostess was so pretty that she didn't need to be anything else, and so modest that she thought everybody wonderful, and seemed to be listening when she wasn't.

The guest of the evening was a large-scale Englishman just back from West Africa. He sat on his hostess's right and presently began telling of what must have been, I am sure, a terrific adventure in the great forest of the Congo.

When he had suggested telling of his experience, our hostess had said, "Oh, do, Mr. Rawlinson!" and as he told it she had sat gazing into his face with every sign of rapt attention. She seemed to be hanging on every word.

So she was—in a way. In her right hand she had a spoon ready to help a silver dish of trifle, and she wanted to be quite sure when Rawlinson had done, so as to give him a spoonful. The little flashes of animation that he saw pass across her features were merely false starts that meant that once or twice she had thought he was through and he wasn't.

With such encouragement Rawlinson carried his story toward its climax with increasing dramatic effect, so much so that the rest of us at the supper table were all listening to him. He was telling how he himself and a single companion were hopelessly lost, at midnight, in the great woods of the Congo, shuddering under the dripping forest, when—so related Rawlinson— "All of a sudden, as we sat there, we heard the most piercing shriek for 'help' echoing through the woods."

Rawlinson paused, and sat back to enjoy the dramatic effect.

Our pretty hostess reached out and helped him to a spoonful of trifle, and said very quietly and comfortably, as if carrying on the topic still further:

"Of course when we go to the woods we always take our own help."

At which, whether it was good manners or not, we all burst out laughing, so much so that our hostess

ooked across to her husband in charming perplexity
and asked:

"Now, what have I said?"

There was something childishly appealing in the
confession, but as her husband just went on laughing,
I explained to her:

"You said nothing. Rawlinson's lost in the woods
on the Congo, but let him stay there. Go on with the
rifle."

ATMOSPHERE

HOTEL keeping, I can assure you, is a highly special-
ized art. Not every man can do it. You have, in a way,
to be born to it. It is a matter of character, and atmosphere. You either have it, or you don't.

Many Montrealers of the older generation will recall the memory of the genial Mr. Klick, the manager
of one of our most select hotels. It was Mr. Klick's
standing illusion that the "guests" were *his* guests, in
the personal sense. "We had your brother George with
us again last week," he would say to me. "It was a
great pleasure to have him." To Mr. Klick, George's
visit was directed personally toward himself, and the
illusion—since life is built up on such—created a certain atmosphere of reality.

Another such I knew for whom a similar illusion
was extended even to the creature comforts that he
dispensed. The old-fashioned bar of the Somerset
House in Toronto, where he presided—a bar glisten-
ing with mahogany and redolent of lemon and spices—

was for him not a hired place of commercial entertainment but a sort of sanctuary where the connoisseur was met and matched by an art equal to the measure of his appreciation.

"I hear you have some new ale out from England, Mr. Hopkins," I once said to him. "May I have a glass of it?"

"Sorry, Mr. Leacock," he said, "I can't serve it to you—not for another three weeks—not fair to the ale, sir, not fair to the ale."

To Mr. Hopkins, ale was a living, breathing creature, with rights and sentiments of its own.

Knowing this of hotel atmosphere, I was interested in being able to witness, a couple of summers ago, the very process by which such an atmosphere is brought into being.

I entered the "rotunda" of one of those pleasant little frame hotels, newly built, that dot the inner channel of the Georgian Bay. When I had duly registered, I said to the proprietor, who seemed to be the only person around:

"You have a charming spot here. Do you get a nice class of people?"

"Very nice class of people," he assured me. "Mostly professional men up from Toronto, men like Judge Barracot who is with us just now."

"Have you good fishing?" I asked.

"Very good, indeed; our guests generally take a guide and go up toward Parry Sound. Judge Barracot was out this morning."

"Do they get many?"

"Generally get a very fair catch. Judge Barracot was saying he got a dozen bass this morning."

From which the proprietor went on to talk of golf and said that the improvised course of nine holes seemed to give excellent satisfaction. Someone, he thought it was Judge Barracot, had gone round yesterday under fifty.

"Will it be possible to get a game of bridge in the evening?" I asked.

"Oh, I don't think that will be any trouble. One of our guests, Judge Barracot, was talking this morning of getting up a table."

"Perhaps," I said, "as I've an hour or so before supper, you might introduce me to one or two of the guests, if you don't mind."

"Why, yes, certainly. Now let me see, I wonder who you'd like to meet. Come with me to the lounge."

He led me from the rotunda into a side room, where an elderly man was seated reading a paper.

"Judge Barracot," he said, "I want you to meet Professor Leacock. . . ."

"You've been here often before?" I asked the Judge.

"No," he said. "I just came up from Toronto yesterday. As far as I know you and I are the only guests; the hotel only opened on Monday."

.   .   .   .

But at any rate we were not left long as the only guests. Even while we were talking I was aware of the entry of a new guest into the rotunda, and through the open door I could hear our host say:

"Oh, yes; our guests are very largely professional men and college men. We have men like Judge Barracot and men like Professor Leacock . . ."

Now don't ask me the nearer address of this little hotel. It would be not good if you did, for it's all booked for summer, as it deserves to be. Atmosphere has settled on it.

FREEDOM OF THOUGHT

IN these days when there is so much discussion of dictatorship and the suppression of free thought, it is well to get any light one can on what free thought and free speech should properly mean.

Now it is generally understood that the people of the Southern States, especially the generation of "the war," whatever their faults may have been, were at least conspicuous for their chivalrous sense of honour and fair play. So I am glad to be able to contribute to the vexed discussion of free thought a personal testimony as to how they look on it in Arkansas.

There came from that State, to spend the summer in my home town, a gallant old Southerner, at that time Attorney General of Arkansas, and a veteran— an ex-general—of the Confederate Army. It was in my earlier days at McGill and I was lecturing on American history, and, when I met General Morsy, it seemed wonderful to me to talk with a man to whom the Civil War was a vivid personal recollection, and who bore the marks of it, in his stilted walk and his stiffened arm.

I took the General out sailing on Lake Couchiching, and the old man sat on the gunwhale of the boat, as easily as on a gun-wagon, but he never saw the waves, and he never felt the wind nor noticed the blue of the cloudless sky, for he was talking of the battle of Shiloh and was telling how Albert Sydney Johnston died. I took him out for a drive—there were no motors then —and he never saw the woods nor noticed the ripening fields of grain, for his talk was of Pemberton's stand at Vicksburg, and before his eyes, as he spoke, the Mississippi rolled below the bluff.

Now it so happened that that summer I received a suggestion about an appointment to the University of Arkansas—one of those tentative half-offers that whisper in the ears of young college lecturers. Naturally I wanted to know about the place, and whether my opinions, as an economist, would be free, would be my own. So I asked General Morsy about it.

"Sir," he said, "if you come to our State, as I hope you may, you will find with us the most complete academic freedom. We make it a point of honour. You can think and talk entirely as you like."

The General paused, and, after a minute's reflection, he added:

"We shall, of course, take it for granted, sir, that you believe in free silver."

.   .   .   .

Simple, isn't it? Solves the whole problem. After all, if a man's salary is good enough, surely he can believe in anything.

HIS BETTER SELF

It is strange the devious ways in which drink affects different men. Some grow quarrelsome, others optimistic and merry, and others again sentimental and reminiscent.

But the oddest form of "bats" or "jags" I ever knew or heard of were those of my old Toronto classmate, Walter McLellan, whose drunks brought on an access of morality.

I was reading the other night in a book on psychology about what is called the "super-consciousness" or the "super-self." It is held that in moments of danger, of emergency, some people rise to another and higher self that never comes to the surface in their daily life. It is argued that drink, too, may at times exercise this effect.

This "super-self" must have been what was wrong with Walter.

I would come at times into his office in the morning—Walter had finished Varsity and was trying to practise law—to find him with his head in his hands in a fit of depression.

"I feel awful," Walter said. "I went into the Dog and Duck last night and had four or five drinks and it started me off."

"What did you do?" I asked.

"I took mother up to the Church of the Redeemer to the choir practice; I was full as a fly—"

"And where did you go after the choir practice?"

"Into the rectory with mother for supper," said

Walter with a groan.

"And after supper?"

"Played chess with the rector—full as a bug."

That was the peculiar nature of Walter's outbreaks. He took it all in one load, like a camel, and lived on it all evening, without any outward sign at all. He never talked much anyway. He himself knew he was "plastered," but the rector didn't.

I remember another afternoon on which Walter went on a terrible bat and took his aunt to the art gallery: and another day when there came to his office a card of invitation from the college to a lecture on palaeontology, and Walter got so full that he went and listened to it.

Xmas always hit him hard. "I made a perfect darn fool of myself with drink yesterday," he said, in telling me about it the day after.

"What did you do, Walter?" I asked.

"I got an awful skate on quite early in the morning over at Clancy's."

"Yes, and what then?"

"I went up to my married sister's house and went to morning service with her and the children—I certainly was soused—and what did I do but give the three children twenty-five dollars each!"

"That's all right, Walter," I said; "it's fine for them."

"Oh, I know," Walter said, "but that wasn't the whole of it. I signed a subscription for a hundred dollars to rebuild the darn chancel."

.   .   .   .

Of course if a man goes downhill like that it can't last forever. Walter's law business was getting all shot to pieces with choir practice and taking his aunt to lectures and his mother to the Church of the Redeemer.

It was clear that his "super-self" was driving Walter to ruin.

His last outbreak practically cleaned him out. He was full all day—at a church committee meeting and with his mother at a lecture and ended by giving his sister a cheque to pay the eldest boy's fees for a year at college.

That ended Walter. He quit his practice and started off for the Yukon in the gold rush of 1898.

Walter got to the Yukon, by the Edmonton trail, safe enough, and within a year we'd heard in Toronto that he had struck it rich and was cleaning up a fortune. But right on the heels of this intelligence came the news that Walter had gone on a terrible bat in Dawson City and lost practically everything in a gift to start a Church of England mission.

After that I heard no more of him. They said he had moved to Colorado or some other mining place.

But in the last number of the magazine of my old college, I saw that under the will of somebody whose name seemed meant for his, the college received a gift of a hundred thousand dollars.

So Walter must have drunk himself to death somewhere.

OH, SLEEP! OH, GENTLE SLEEP!

SLEEP is a great thing, there's no doubt of it. And it's always at its best when you take it at an improper time, as forbidden fruit. That is why sleep is so beautiful during a sermon, and why college students crowd into classes on philosophy.

Sleep is also partly a natural gift.

The most naturally gifted sleeper I ever knew was my classmate of long ago at Toronto, Walter Allen. Walter had such a bright mind that he could sleep for sixteen hours a day and still have mind enough for everything. He took a double course in Greek and metaphysics, impossible for a light sleeper. Later on he rose to eminence on the bench and bar of Illinois. The Americans admired his power of sifting evidence in court with his eyes shut.

But I'm telling now about how Walter went from Toronto to New York for the Yacht Race—the American Cup Race—between the *Defender* and the *Valkyrie*. That must have been back in the nineties.

To save money—we were all hard up in the nineties—Walter took no Pullman but sat up awake all night, a thing he hadn't done since he was born. This economic travel brought him among the first on the tugboat that you took to see the race. It was not to start for an hour, a breezy morn of wind and sun, with sleep in every breath of it. Walter found a huge coil of rope in a sheltered corner astern; just the place for a snooze; time enough to get a good place at the bow later on.

He lay down. Sleep breathed upon him. He had a confused idea of motion, of sea breezes, of trampling feet—and then a man, a deck hand, bent over him and shook him and said:

"You'll have to get up, please, sir. We're back at the dock in New York."

Next morning when he reached Toronto someone asked:

"Who won the Yacht Race, Walter? I forgot to look in the paper."

"So did I," said Walter.

EPILOGUE

Bass Fishing on Lake Simcoe with Jake Gaudaur

(*It ought to be the privilege of an author to reserve some part of his book as his own, and to put into it whatever he likes. Especially in the present volume, of which the earlier part contains so much that is controversial and might arouse anger and disagreement, is it fitting to end with a discourse on fishing where no anger is and where disagreement is only on the surface—which in fishing is of no account. S.L.)*

BASS FISHING ON LAKE SIMCOE WITH
JAKE GAUDAUR

AMONG the pleasant memories of my life is the recollection of my fishing days on Ontario's Lake Simcoe
with Jake Gaudaur—little excursions that extended
over twenty or twenty-five years. If you don't know
the name of Jake Gaudaur it only means that you were
born fifty years too late. Half a century ago Jake was
for several years the champion oarsman of the world
—a title won on the Thames at Henley. In those days,
before motor-cars and aeroplanes, rowing was one of
the big interests of the nations, and Jake Gaudaur was
a hero to millions who had never seen him. The fact
that his name was pronounced exactly as Good-Oar
helped to keep it easily in mind.

Jake was of mixed French and Indian descent but
belonged in the Lake Simcoe country and English had
always been his language—the kind we use up there,
not the kind that they use at Oxford. I can talk both,
but the Lake Simcoe kind is easier and, for fishing, far
better. It cuts out social distinction. Jake was a magnificent figure of a man; he stood nicely over six feet
in his stocking feet—the only way we ever measure
people up there. He was broad in the shoulders,
straight as a lath, and till the time when he died, just
short of eighty, he could pick up the twenty-pound
anchor of his motor boat and throw it round like a

tack-hammer. Jake—standing erect in the bow of his motor boat and looking out to the horizon, his eyes shaded with his hand—might have stood for the figure of Oshkosh, war chief of the Wisconsin Indians.

When Jake's championship days were over he came back to Canada and "kept hotel" in Sudbury. That was the thing for champions to do; in the unregenerate days of the old bar, thousands of people spent five cents on a drink just to say they had talked with Jake Gaudaur. I wish that retired professors could open up a bar. It must be a great thing to be an ex-champion, or a quintuplet, and never have to work.

So Jake made his modest pile and then came back to our part of the country, the Lake Simcoe district, and set up at the Narrows, at the top end of the lake, as a professional fisherman, taking out parties on the lake for bass fishing.

Now, who hasn't seen Lake Simcoe has never seen a lake at all. Lake Simcoe on a July morning—the water, ruffled in wavelets of a blue and green and silver, as clear as never was: the sky of the purest blue with great clouds white and woolly floating in it! Just the day for fishing!—every day is, for the enthusiast.

The lake is just right in size to be what a lake ought to be—twenty to thirty miles across in any direction—so that there's always a part of the horizon open where you can't see the land. The shore is all irregular with bays and "points" and islands and shoals, so that any roads thereabouts are away back from the water and the shore line of trees and sand and stone look much as Champlain saw it three hundred years ago

Over it in the summer air of July there hovers an atmosphere of unbroken peace. When I think of it I cannot but contrast it with the curse that lies over Europe where mountain lakes are scarped and galleried for guns, and every church steeple on their shores a range and target. I wish I could take Hitler and Mussolini out bass fishing on Lake Simcoe. They'd come **back** better men—or they'd never come back.

.   .   .   .

So here we are at ten o'clock in the morning helping Jake load the stuff out of our car into his motor boat! Notice that—ten o'clock. None of that fool stuff about starting off at daylight. You get over that by the time you're forty. The right time to start off bass fishing is when you're good and ready to. And when I say ten o'clock, I really mean about ten-thirty. We just call it ten o'clock and when you look at your watch after you're actually started, it's always ten-thirty, or not much past it. Anyway there's no finer time in the day on the water than ten-thirty—still all the freshness of the morning and all the day in front of you—half way between windy and calm with little ruffled waves in the sunlight, and a cool breeze, partly made by the boat itself.

As for the bass, they bite as well at any one time as at any other. The idea that they bite at daylight and don't bite after lunch is just a myth. They bite when they're ready to; the only reason they don't bite after lunch is that the fishermen are asleep till three.

Jake's boat is no "power" boat, to hit up twenty-five miles an hour. That fool stuff came to our lakes later

and is out of keeping with bass fishing. Jake's is a big
roomy open boat with a front part for Jake and a big
open part at the back where we sit—a broad stern seat
with leather cushions and wicker arm-chairs on a linoleum floor. Solid comfort. No rough stuff for us;
we're not sailors. And no cover to keep off the sun—
who cares a darn about the sun when you're fishing—
and nothing to keep off the wind—let it come; and no
protection against the rain. It *won't* rain. Any man
who thinks it's going to rain shouldn't go fishing.

"Will it rain, Jake?"

"I don't think so, Professor; not with that sky."

We've gone through that little opening dialogue, I
suppose, a hundred times. That's the beauty of bass
fishing: always doing the same things in the same way
with the same old jokes and the same conversation.

"I was thinking we might go out and try the big
rock at McCrae's point first, Professor," says Jake.

Seeing that we've never done anything else in twenty
years, it seems a likely thing to do.

This gives us two miles to go—down from the Narrows to the open lake and then sideways across to the
first point. For me this is always the best part of the
day—the cool fresh air, the anticipation better than
reality, the settling into our wicker chairs and lighting
up our pipes, with the stuff all properly stowed around
us, the fishing-gear, the lunch and the box with the
soda on ice. Not that we take a drink at this time of
the day. Oh, no! We're all agreed that you don't need
a drink on a beautiful fine morning at ten-thirty—unless perhaps just as an exception today because it's

uch a damn fine day that you feel so good you'd like
drink. There are two reasons for taking a drink
hen you're out bass fishing—one, because you feel so
ood, and the other—because you don't feel so good.
o perhaps this morning, "Eh what?"

"Well, just a starter."

"Jake, can I pass you along a horn?"

"Thanks, Professor, I don't mind."

There are four of us, mostly, apart from Jake, so
. takes most of the time of the run to mix up and
erve the drinks. I am thinking here especially of one
arty, though really it was just like all the others.
'here was my brother George and George Rapley,
he bank manager (a tear to his kind memory), and
'harlie Janes, the railroad man of a Lake Simcoe
own. George Rapley always came because he could
sh, and Charlie Janes because he *couldn't*. You may
ave noticed that bank managers are always good fish-
rmen; it's something in their profession, I think, a
ind of courtesy, that gets the fish. And I am sure that
verybody who goes bass fishing will agree that to
nake the party right you need one fellow who *can't*
sh. In fact in any bass fishing party of friends who
o out often together, there is always one who is cast
or the part of not knowing how to fish. No matter
ow often he's been out, he's not supposed to know
nything about fishing and he good-naturedly accepts
he role. If he loses a fish, that's supposed to be be-
ause he didn't know how to land it; if *we* lose a fish
t's supposed to be because it was *impossible* to land it.

It's these little mutual understandings that fit life to
gether.

. . . .

So almost before the "horn" is finished, here we ar
bearing down on the big rock off McCrae's point. It'
nearly a quarter of a mile from shore and six fee
under water, but Jake steers to it like a taxi to a hote
door. The anchor goes down with a splash, our swing
on it timed to throw us right over the rock! There i
is! See it—big as a wagon!—and in another minut
down go the baited lines trailing to go under the edg
of the great rock.

This is the great moment of fishing, the first minut
with the lines down—tense, exhilarating. It's alway
the same way—either something big happens, or noth
ing. Perhaps—bing! the lines are no sooner down tha
a bass is hooked—by Charlie Janes, of course—jus
like the luck of the darned fool! And while he's stil
hauling on it—biff! there's another one—and Jake, i
seems, has quietly landed a third one when the othe
two were plunging round. With which there's such a
period of excitement and expectation that it's nearl
three quarters of an hour before you realize that thos
three fish are all there are—or rather *two* fish: Georg
Rapley lost his—too bad! he was playing it so beau
tifully. Charlie Janes, the darned old fool, flung hi
over the side of the boat, right slap into the ice-box

Or else—the other alternative—the lines go dow
and nothing happens.

In either case we fish on and on under the rock til
excitement fades into dullness, and dullness into dea

certainty. That's *all*. At last someone says, "I guess they ain't biting here any more." Notice *"They're not biting";* we never say, *"they're not here."* Any man who says, as I have heard some of our odd guests say, "Oh, hell, there are no fish here," is not fit to be brought again. The only theory on which bass fishing can be maintained as a rational pastime is that the bass are *everywhere*—all the time. But they won't bite. The wind may be wrong, or the air just too damp, or too dry, or too much sun, or not enough—it's amazing how little will start a bass not biting. But the cause must always be one that can change in five minutes, or with a move of five yards. These beliefs are to a fisherman what faith is to a Christian.

"We might try out past Strawberry Island," says Jake. This means a change farther out, right out in the open water of the lake with the whole horizon of wind and wave and sun open for twenty miles all around to the south. This is not exactly a shoal. The bottom of the lake drops here from twelve feet to thirty feet of water—like the side of a hill. Jake explains it all fresh every time, and he makes each new spot seem so different and so likely that we go at each with new hope eternal. If we don't get any fish as each half hour stop goes by, Jake tells the story of how he and I fished once and never had a bite till after sundown and then caught thirty-three bass in half an hour off McGinnis's reef. "You mind that evening, Professor?" he says (to "mind" a thing is to remember it). "It was thirty-three, wasn't it?"

"Thirty-four I think, Jake," I answer, and he says,

"Well, mebbee it was." We've brought those fish up a little every year.

Or else Jake tells the story of the young girl from Toledo who came up with her father and had never been fishing before and never even in a motor boat, and it was a caution how many she caught. This story, of course, conveys the idea that if inexperienced fishers, like the young lady from Toledo, can catch fish, experienced people like ourselves could hardly expect to.

．　　．　　．　　．　　．　　．　　．

Then all of a sudden as it always seems, comes the idea of lunch—all of a sudden everybody hungry and ready for it. And does ever food taste better than out in the wind and sun in a motor boat?—salmon sandwiches, cold chicken in a salad, chunks of home-made bread, mustard pickles; all eaten partly off a plate and partly with your fingers and with bottled ale to wash it down.

People who go fishing but are not real fishermen land on shore for lunch, light a fire and, I believe, even cook the fish caught. Some of them go so far as to have a game of poker or, in extreme cases of mental derangement, go for a swim. All of this to a proper fisherman is just deplorable, just lunacy. The true fisherman eats right in the boat with the lines still hanging in the water. There seems to be a sort of truce during lunch time; I never knew a bass to touch a hook till it's over. But lunch on the other hand isn't hurried. It's just eaten in the natural way. You put into your mouth all it will hold; then eat it; then start again

Eating in the open air knows no satiety, no indigestion.

The whole point is that the longest day is all too short for fishing, and no one who really loves bass fishing can bear the thought of knocking off from it even for an hour. As a matter of fact, we *do* take time off but we never admit it. For there also came in our fishing with Jake a drowsy part of the day when we took a sleep. Not that we ever called it that deliberately. The sleep was just a sort of accident. A little while after we'd eaten all the lunch we could hold Jake would say: "I thought we might go and try for a spell down round the corner of that shoal—just off that way apiece. You mind we was there before?"

"Yes, sure, I remember it, Jake."

The place is a sort of convenient little nook among the shoals—nothing showing on top of the water. We always reckoned as if the bottom were in sight. It had the advantage that the waves couldn't reach it, because of the shallows, and it was always quiet, and no fish ever came there. Jake could anchor the boat where there were just enough waves to rock the boat gently and just enough light breeze to murmur a lullaby— and with the two-o'clock sun to make you pull your straw panama away over your eyes, a man seated like that in a wicker chair, with two pounds of sandwiches and six ounces of whisky in him, is as drowsy as a flower nodding on its stem, and asleep in five minutes. The lines dangle in the water; there is no conversation, no sound but the breeze and the lapping of the little waves. Up in front we could see only Jake's broad back, but there was slumber in every line of it.

It didn't matter who woke first. After about an hour anybody could straighten up and say: "By Jove, I believe I was almost asleep. Were you?" And the others would answer, "Darn near!" And then Jake would say, as if he'd never stopped talking, "I was thinking we might go out and try the dry shoal."

This rouses us to a new search for bass, hither and thither half a mile, a mile, at a time. Even then we are only covering one corner of Lake Simcoe. The lake is just big enough to seem illimitable.

Bass fishing on Lake Simcoe is not like the bass fishing you can get a hundred miles north of it, on the rivers in the bush, out of easy reach. Up there it's no come-and-go business in a day; you must stay at least two nights. You catch one hundred bass in the first day and the next day you don't even keep them; you throw them back. The third day you hate the stinking things; a bass two days dead, with its skin discoloured, would sicken even a cannibal.

Not so Lake Simcoe. There are just not enough bass, just never too many—some dead, dull days without any—they're there, but they won't bite. But even on the deadest, dullest day, always the hope of a strike.

You might wonder, if you don't know the life, why the afternoon never gets dreary, what there can be to talk about—especially among men often and always out together on the same ground. That's just ignorance. In bass fishing there are vast unsettled problems, to be discussed forever. For example, do you need to "play" a bass, or is that just a piece of damn nonsense imitated out of salmon fishing? The school to which I belong holds that "playing" a bass is just a way of losing it. What you need is a steel rod with the last section taken out and an "emergency tip" put in—making a short firm rod about six feet long. When the bass nibbles, *wait*—then wait some more—then strike—with such power as to drive the hook right through his head—then shorten the line—not with a reel; that's too slow—haul it in beside the reel with your left hand and hold it firm with your right—shove the rod close to the water, if need be *under* the water —by that means the bass *can't* jump out of the water, there isn't line enough—drag him against his will till someone else holds the net—and in he comes.

Contrast this with the artistic "playing" of fish that *looks* so skilful—paying out line—the fish leaping in the air thirty feet from the boat—and all that show stuff—only good for a picture book!

Now can't you see that the discussion of that point alone can fill an afternoon?

Personally I am always an extremist for a short rod and rapid action—the bass right in the boat in twenty seconds. I think that in his heart Jake Gaudaur agreed with this. It's the way all Indians fish and always have. But Jake's calling demanded compromise. He favored both sides. Rapley, like all bankers, played a fish as they play a customer with a loan, taking it in gradually.

.   .   .   .

We always knew that the afternoon was closing to evening when Jake said:

"Suppose we go out and try that big rock inside

McGinnis's reef. You mind, Professor? The place where you caught all them bass, that night; thirty-four, wasn't it?"

"Yes, or thirty-five, Jake. I'm not sure. Let's try it."

This sunken rock is the triumph of Jake's navigation of the lake. It's a mile from even the nearest point of land, and sunk six feet down. Beside it the big rock at McCrae's is child's play. That one you can find if you keep on looking for it. This one, never. It's all very well to say that you can do it with "bearings"; any amateur yachtsman that ever wore Panama pants will tell you that. But try it. Try to get bearings that are good at all hours and all lights and shadows on the shores, good in rain and good in mist, and you soon see where you are—or are not.

Jake, erect at the bow as he steers, is as straight as Oshkosh; the boat gathers speed in a curve that picks up one of the bearings and then straight as a pencil line over the water for a mile—then a stop with a reversed engine, without a turn, or the bearings would be lost, and there we are—right over the rock. In a clear light it's as plain as day, but on a dull day you can just make it out, a great rock sunk in a wide basin of water for the bass to get in.

Here we try our final luck. We can't leave. If the bass are there (I mean if they are biting) it's too good to leave. If we don't get a bite, we just *can't* leave.

We haven't realized it, but the afternoon has all gone. The sun is setting behind the hills on the west side of the lake. Just before it goes its beams light up for a moment the windows of unseen farm-houses ten miles the other side of us—and then, before we know it, the sun is gone. But we can't leave. It's still broad daylight yet.

"There's two or three hours good fishing yet, Jake, eh?"

"All of that, Professor."

Somehow it seems as if the day were suddenly all gone. "Have another horn, Jake?" Surely that'll hold the daylight a little, giving Jake a horn. Anyway we can't leave. The light is fading a little. A cold wind begins to move across the lake; the water seems to blacken under its touch as the boat swings to it.

"The wind's kind o' gone round," says Jake. "I thought it would." It's not surprising. The wind has gone round and the air turned chill after sundown every evening of the sixty years I've known Lake Simcoe. But we can't leave. Charlie Janes has had a bite—or says he has. We never take Charlie's word, of course, as really good; he may have caught in a crack of rock. But Rapley thinks he had a nibble. That's better evidence. So we stay on—and on—till the dark has fallen, the shores have all grown dim and then vanished and the north-west wind is beginning to thump the waves on the bow of the anchored boat.

"I guess, gentlemen, it's about time to pull up," says Jake. If we had caught fifteen or twenty bass he'd have said, "Boys, I guess it's about time to quit." But "gentlemen" brings us back to the cold cruel reality.

So the anchor is up and the motor boat at its full power set for home. It's quite rough on the water now;

the boat slaps into the waves and sends the spray fly-
ing clear astern to where we have our chairs huddled
together, back to the wind. It's dark too. You have to
use a flash-light to open the soda for the "consolation
drinks" that mark the end of the fishing.

"Have a horn, Jake?"

"Thanks, Professor."

Jake, with his oil clothes on, can't leave the wheel
now; he sits there all in the spray with one hand for
steering and one for the drink.

. . . .

It's amazing how a lake like Lake Simcoe can
change—a few hours ago a halcyon paradise, still and
calm—and now with the night and the wind gathering
over it—

"Oh, well, Jake knows the way," and anyway it's
only three miles till we'll be in shelter of the Narrows!
—Whew! that was a corker, that wave! "Here, put
these newspapers behind your back, Charlie, they'll
keep off the spray."

Just enough of this to give one a slight feeling of
night and mimic danger—and then, in no great time,
for the distance is short, we round into the shelter of
the Narrows with just a mile of water, smoother and
smoother, to run.

All different it looks from the morning; what you
see now is just lights—a perplexing galaxy of lights,
white and green and red here and there on the unseen
shore—and great flares of moving white light that
must be the motors on the highway.

"What's the red light away up, Jake?"

"That's the one above the railway bridge." We always ask Jake this and when he answers we know we are close in. The water suddenly is quite smooth, a current running with us—the summer cottages and docks come in sight, with "young fellers" and girls in canoes and the sound of a radio somewhere discussing war in Europe.

We're back in the world again, landed at Jake's dock with a little crowd of loafers and boys standing round to see "how many fish Jake got"—not us, *Jake*. We unload the boat and take a look at the string of fish. "Let's see that big one that Rapley caught, eh?" But where is it? Surely it can't be this small dirty-looking flabby thing—I'm afraid it is.

We divide the fish. Jake won't take any. We try to work them off on one another. Fishermen want *fishing*, never fish—and end by slinging them into the car all in one box. "Well, we certainly had a fine day; good night, Jake." And another fishing day has gone—now never to return.

I can only repeat, in tribute to a fine memory, "Good night, Jake."

FINIS